COWTOWN

Cattle Trails And

West Bottom Tales

Published by Woodneath Press
8900 NE Flintlock Rd.
Kansas City, MO 64157

Cover design and typography: Cody Croan

The front cover image is from a series of vintage postcards issued by the Union Pacific Railway, depicting scenes from the states served by the railroad. Its use was graciously authorized by the Union Pacific with assistance from Tracey L. Howerton, senior manuscript specialist, University of Missouri – Kansas City.

The back cover image is titled, "Old Chisholm Trail" by Clara McDonald Williams. The original was painted in 1952 oil on panel, 24x36 1/2. Permission to use this image was granted from the Roland P. Murdock Collection, Wichita Art Museum, Wichita, KS.

Publisher's Cataloguing-in-Publication
(Provided by Woodneath Press: A Program of Mid-Continent Public Library)

Matheny, Edward T. (Edward Taylor)
    Cowtown : Cattle Trails and West Bottom Tales / by Ed Matheny, Jr.
    p. cm.
    LCCN
    ISBN 978-1-942337-00-3

    1. Stockyards – Missouri -- Kansas City – History   2. Livestock – Missouri – History 3. Cattle Trade – Missouri – History. 1. Title.

977.8411

COWTOWN

Cattle Trails And West Bottom Tales

TABLE OF CONTENTS

FOREWORD 1
INTRODUCTION 2
FROM TRAILS TO TRACKS 4
STOCKYARDS 10
THE PACKERS 14
THE COWBOY 17
THE IRISH 20
JAMES PENDERGAST 22
BOSTON BRAHMANS AND BELFAST BUTCHERS 27
PROGRESS 29
THE LIVESTOCK COMMISSION MERCHANTS 31
OTHER EARLY BUSINESSES 35
FROM OXEN TO CABLE CARS 40
RED WHEAT AND RED MEAT 44
STRAWBERRY HILL 48
FERDINAND THE BULL AND OTHER HAZARDS 53
FLOODS 55
THE SHIPLEY SADDLERY 58
MAJOR CHANGES 62
UNION STATION 64
FIRES!!! 65
THE AMERICAN ROYAL 68
SOSLAND PUBLISHING COMPANY 72
STOCKYARD ACTIVITY 75
THE PLATTS 80
KANEY'S KID 83
THE FRATERNITY 90
THE DILLINGHAMS 93
A MISSOURI MULE IN THE MOVIES 98
EVERYTHING WAS UP TO DATE IN KANSAS CITY 99
WORLD WAR II 103
BILL HORNER 107
OLE FERD OWEN 108
ORGANIZE! 110
SOME AMERICAN ROYAL SUPPORTERS 111
THE LIVESTOCK EXCHANGE BUILDING AND "THE OX\ 115
THE FLOOD OF 1951 117
TWO STOCKYARD VISITORS OF NOTE 125
YOUTHFUL MEMORIES 128
LOULA LONG COMBS 133
TIME RUNS OUT 135
R. CROSBY KEMPER JR. 138
POSSUM TROT AND BARBECUE 140
THE END 144
LEGACIES 146
WHAT'S NEXT? 150
OF JACKPOTS AND NUT FRIES 155
CONCLUSION 158

ACKNOWLEDGEMENTS...159
ILLUSTRATIONS 161
ABOUT THE AUTHOR 162
INDEX...163

C O W T O W N

Cattle Trails And West Bottom Tales

FOREWORD

Future generations will owe a big "thank you" to Ed Matheny for telling the story about Kansas City's early history and largest business - the stockyards.

My father Jay remarked more than once that he heard J.C. Nichols say that there wouldn't be a Country Club Plaza if there hadn't been the stockyards.

At one point on those 200 acres on both sides of the Kaw River over 100 years ago, 80% of all Kansas City business was located in what some call our West Bottoms. Over a dozen railroads came here. The stockyards were the heartbeat of a large "shopping mall" for all the folks buying and selling their animals and then needing related farm products and supplies in nearby stores.

Following the Civil War, Kansas City might not have grown if not for millions of cheap Texas cattle, the Abilene, Kansas rail head, the Hannibal Bridge, the immigrant workers walking to the packing plants from Strawberry Hill, and the railroad yards that took our products to Chicago and on East.

167,000 head of animals came in 1871. In 1908, only 37 years later, we had 100,000 head per day generating $1 million daily. And 350,000 Missouri mules went off to fight World War 1.

Fiscal integrity and personal honesty were stockyard trademarks.

The stockyards started the American Royal and the Future Farmers of America.

The 1951 flood ultimately closed the stockyards' doors, although it took another 40 years for that to happen. However, the Golden Ox where the "steak was born" is still going strong.

John Dillingham

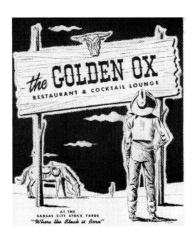

COWTOWN

Cattle Trails And West Bottom Tales

INTRODUCTION

Kansas City began with a settlement on the Missouri River. As the number of settlers grew, some of them followed a water-level route along the river's south bank rather than climb the bluffs hemming in their Westport Landing. The journey of most ended near the junction of the Missouri River with the Kansas, or Kaw, River, in an area that became known as the West Bottoms.

The fledgling community along the river came perilously close to adopting the name "Possum Trot" but was saved from this ignominy by the historians in their midst. The latter recognized that the indigenous Kansa Indians, their predecessors in the area, were deserving of recognition and so the settlement became the City of Kansas.

The residents of the City of Kansas were joined by others. The Corps of Discovery of Lewis & Clark just passed through, as did wagon train pioneers, Chisholm Trail cowboys, Freedom Trail escaping slaves, and overnight guests at the Blossom House hotel. But the Armours came to stay and build a city, as did the Soslands, the Dillinghams, and many more.

Pioneer Mother Memorial in Penn Valley Park, by Alexander Phimister Proctor (1927)
Donated by Howard Vanderslice
Noll Postcard Collection

C O W T O W N

Cattle Trails And West Bottom Tales

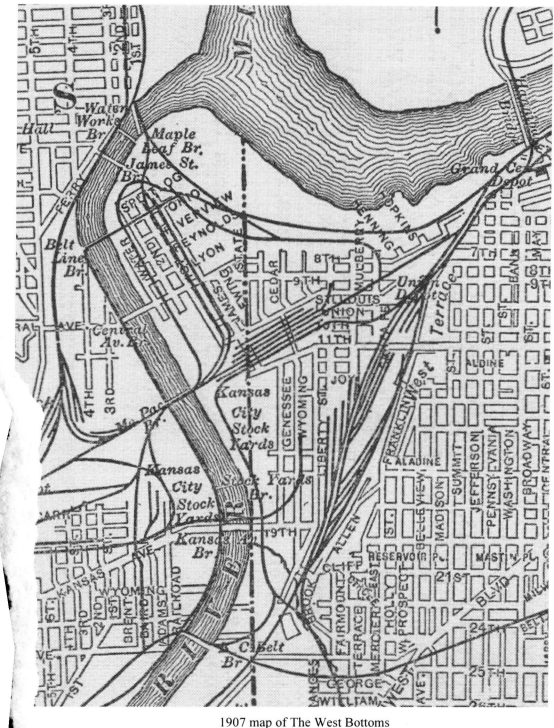

1907 map of The West Bottoms
Based upon Gazetteer of Cities and Towns of the World; Dodd, Mead & Co.

C O W T O W N

Cattle Trails And West Bottom Tales

FROM TRAILS TO TRACKS

Conquistador Hernando Cortes brought to the New World the long-horned cattle of Spain. The vacas flourished in the barren lands of northern Mexico, where the first vaqueros (cowboys) were Spanish-speaking and wore wide-brimmed sombreros to provide shade (sombra) for their faces. According to Alton Pryor (Cowboys; The End of the Trail, Stagecoach Publishing, 2006) it was in 1690 that the first herd of longhorns was driven north from Mexico to the land that would become Texas.

The earliest of the major cattle trails from Texas to northern railheads was the Shawnee Trail, long used by Indians in raiding and hunting. The Shawnee Indian Mission buildings in Fairway, Kansas recall those early years. The Mission opened in 1839 and constitutes a U.S. National Historic Landmark. Texas cattle drovers began in 1840 to follow the Shawnee Trail to its terminal in Kansas City.

Shawnee Indian Mission; Fairway, KS
Photo by Steve Noll

The Civil War obstructed cattle movements for four years, and after that war came to an end Te was overrun with longhorns. There was great demand for beef cattle in the east, and supply abundant in the Lone Star State. To remedy that, cattle drives were once again instituted. As the the gauntlet of the great cattle trails, drovers had to deal with Comanche Indians, stampedes, pi fires, and cattle rustlers. And their herds included mean longhorn bulls, malevolent creatures long, sharp horns. The drovers' exploits gave rise to much of the cowboy legend. The best kn post-Civil War cattle trail was the Chisholm Trail, named for Jesse Chisholm. Chisholm was a l breed trader whose father was Scotch and whose mother was a Cherokee.

The Chisholm Trail ended in Abilene, Kansas, 170 miles west of Kansas City. Joseph Geiting Mc(a young man from Illinois who is sometimes called the father of Kansas City's cattle industry, bui

COWTOWN

Cattle Trails And West Bottom Tales

Abilene a shipping yard to receive and hold cattle, and load them aboard railroad cars. Abilene became the cattle round-up site for the entire southwest.

Joseph McCoy – Founder of the Chisholm Trail
Photo from "Riders of the Chisholm Trail", by James W. Parker

According to James W. Parker:

> "Joe McCoy masterminded all the arrangements that lured thousands and thousands of longhorns from the impoverished brush country of southern Texas, through the raw lands of Indian Territory, to the promising railhead of Abilene." Riders of the Chisholm Trail by James W. Parker, volume 2, edited by Margaret Chisholm Tulp.

Parker dedicated his book to the American cowboy who was a drover. "At his best he was a hero: intelligent, bold, stout of heart and strong of build. At his worst he was still a colorful character, and he sure knew his longhorns."

****

Riverboats brought passengers and freight to the Landing that became Kansas City. One riverboat was the Arabia. That sunken ship was discovered buried 45 feet deep in a cornfield. Once part of the meandering Missouri River channel, the cornfield at the time of discovery was a half-mile away from the river.

The ship's cargo is on display today in the Arabia Steamboat Museum, 400 Grand Blvd., in the historic City Market complex of Kansas City, Missouri. "Treasure in a Cornfield" by Greg Hawley is for sale at the Museum and describes the discovery and excavation of the Arabia that ended in 1989. The result is the Museum's collection of pre-Civil War artifacts, the largest ever discovered.

The Arabia sank in 1856, striking a submerged walnut tree near Parkville, Missouri, shortly after unloading freight at Westport Landing. Hundreds of Missouri River riverboats suffered the same fate.

C O W T O W N

Cattle Trails And West Bottom Tales

A crowd gathers at the foot of Main Street in 1880 to greet passengers
arriving on a Missouri River steamboat.
Missouri Valley Room Photo

Wood-burning, steam-powered locomotives replaced the riverboats. In 1864, the Kansas Pacific Railway entered Kansas City, followed by the Missouri Pacific Railroad in 1865. A later Kansas Pacific Railway ad for "the old established and popular Texas Stock route" touted good grazing, plentiful water, perfect shipping facilities, free yards and low rates in Abilene. O. James Hazlett, "Cattle Marketing in the American Southwest: The Rise of the Kansas City Commission Merchant in the Nineteenth Century," Kansas History, a Journal of the Central Plains 18 (Summer 1995) page 101.

The initial shipment of Texas cattle to Kansas City from Abilene was in 1867. That year, a railroad depot and a small hotel, the State Line House, were erected in the Kansas City West Bottoms.

In 1869, completion of the Hannibal Bridge across the powerful Missouri River, permitting the linkage of Kansas City to Chicago and the urban northeast, was the final unit in the formation of a renowned stockyard and packinghouse center in the West Bottoms and the evolution of Kansas City from small community to big city.

COWTOWN

Cattle Trails And West Bottom Tales

Octave Chanute's Hannibal Bridge, under construction
Missouri Valley Room Photo

Four years before completion of the Hannibal Bridge, the Kansas City Journal of Commerce prophesied that the city's business would move from its base on the Missouri River levee to the flat lands of the West Bottoms. In anticipation, the City Council of Kansas City, Missouri issued bonds to open Third, Fourth, Fifth and Twelfth Streets from the city's commercial district into the Bottoms.

On July 3, 1869, the first Hannibal & St. Joseph Railroad engine crossed the bridge. As predicted, the new bridge routed rail traffic to the West Bottoms, dedicating the bottoms area to railroad use and to industry relying upon rail service.

C O W T O W N

Cattle Trails And West Bottom Tales

Kansas City's First Railroad Station

Kansas City Star Photo

In 1870, the Hannibal & St. Joseph erected a small frame station on Union Avenue. Soon other railroads crossed the Hannibal Bridge into Kansas City, taking advantage of its bridges and railroad connections. Commercial slaughter of the vast Western buffalo herds began, and among the first products that the railroads brought to Kansas City in sizable numbers were buffalo bones. The skeletons of millions of bison were hauled from the prairies and converted into fertilizer and buttons. Many railroads listed these bones as their major articles for eastbound traffic. Buffalo pelts and leather could be marketed at a profit also. In 1870 a process was developed for converting buffalo hide into commercial leather. The following year J. H. Dubois, a dealer in hides, pelts and furs, opened a business in the West Bottoms at 1424 St. Louis Avenue, the "Dubois hide house."

A mountain of buffalo bones, c.1880.
Burton Historical Collection Detroit Public Library

C O W T O W N

Cattle Trails And West Bottom Tales

Cattle on the Trail From Texas

Twenty Years of Kansas City's Live Stock and Traders, Pearl Printing Company, Kansas City, Missouri, 1893, from the library of John Dillingham

COWTOWN

Cattle Trails And West Bottom Tales

STOCKYARDS

At first, all cattle were merely transferred to other railroads on arrival in Kansas City, for shipment east. Then, in 1870, Colonel L. V. Morse, Superintendent of the Hannibal & St. Joseph Railroad, fenced in a few acres of land and erected rickety temporary pens where cattle could be unloaded, fed and watered. Colonel Morse also installed some Fairbanks scales, a crucial addition.

There came next an exchange building at 12th Street and State Line. Exchange activities were not new to the area — for many years, trappers, hunters, and farmers had met here to swap grain and livestock, and Indians exchanged valuable furs for tobacco, whiskey, and sugar. Now the exchanges could be conducted in a structure which, though consisting of only 24 square feet and lacking facilities for comfort, did keep out the rain and cold.

Drawing of first exchange building, 1871
Twenty Years Photo

Other improvements came quickly, and the Union Stock Yards officially opened on June 1, 1871. There was an announcement of the event in the Kansas City Journal of Commerce on June 4, 1871.

"As the cattle trade of this city is an element of its prosperity, all items pertaining to it are of great interest.

"The Union Stock Yards are now completed and ready for the reception of cattle, and in condition to receive 300 cars of stock per day, which capacity can be doubled or trebled at short notice.

"Unloading tracks and platforms have been provided for the KPRR, the Atchison, Topeka & Santa Fe RR, and the Fort Scott & Gulf roads; and standing tracks and chutes for eastern roads terminating here giving the shipper choice of the following roads...

COWTOWN

Cattle Trails And West Bottom Tales

"In addition to the above the plans are now drawn and contracts are let to build, on the grounds, a grand stock exchange, for the benefit of drovers, traders and visitors, and to be finished very soon. Besides all commercial conveniences, including a business office, there will be connected with the building a restaurant, so that dealers and others can devote their entire time to the yard if necessary.

"The superintendent of the yard, Mr. Jerome Smith, will have lists of all arrivals and departures, and will furnish all other needed information to inquiries. In a few words, the Union Stock Yards are designed to afford every facility for the cattle trade of this city, which is now immense and worthy of the attention of all persons engaged in the livestock business, whether residents of this city or elsewhere. Thus, Kansas City is wheeling into line with all the other great Western markets, and very soon will have all her business so systemized that the rapid accumulation of wealth will be here." Copy of announcement provided courtesy of Alan Rogers, stockyards historian.

1872 image of Texas cattle in Kansas City Union Stock Yards.
Photo courtesy of Alan Rogers

"View of portion of Union Stock Yards after one year of operation. Note the 'rangy' type cattle being inspected by buyers of the day perched atop the fence in right foreground." Alan Rogers.

The editor and owner of the Journal of Commerce, Robert T. Van Horn, was a shameless booster and prodigious producer of articles and pamphlets to lure new residents to Kansas City. He became one of the city's prominent leaders in several capacities — postman, mayor, state senator, Congressman and tax collector.

Very active in Republican politics on the national level for many years, Van Horn deserved much of the credit for the political maneuvers and resulting Congressional approval of a Kansas City site for the

Cattle Trails And West Bottom Tales

Hannibal Bridge. His Independence, Missouri estate, Honeywood, is the site of Van Horn High School.

The "Union Stock Yards" name only lasted three months, replaced by "Kansas Stockyards", probably to avoid confusion with the Chicago yards of the same name.

Photo courtesy of Alan Rogers

"From my own collection, one of the earliest known photographs taken at Kansas City, an 1873 cabinet card of a portion of the Kansas Stockyards, believed to have been taken in September. In the foreground is a small group of steers, which were driven up the trail from Texas to Abilene, Kansas in drives of 1871. They were owned by Kansas City livestock trader John B. Hunter and his son Lem…Photos and tangible items related to the Stockyards during its first few years are in short supply." Alan Rogers.

C O W T O W N

Cattle Trails And West Bottom Tales

1872 Exchange
Twenty Years Photo

An immediate improvement to the exchange shelter was completion of the second story, with commission firms occupying six small offices separated by picket fences in the new space. These improvements meant that weights no longer had to be the conjecture of buyers and sellers. In the years that followed, fewer cattle were sent on to other markets.

The Fairbanks scales, installed by Colonel Morse, employed a system of levers that achieved accurate weighing results and were installed in a pit, placing the sale platform level with the ground.

****

There were also barbers. "So many barbers set up chairs in the West Bottoms, lathering up drovers after three months on the trail, that one local newspaper featured a regular column called The Barbers on its front page." Filthy Rich by Rick Montgomery, Kansas City Star, November 23, 1997.

COWTOWN

Cattle Trails And West Bottom Tales

THE PACKERS

The first Kansas City packing plants were small with limited capacity. The packers had to forage in the countryside for the livestock needed for their plants. With the formation of the Kansas Stockyards Company this changed; the newly organized stockyards provided a steady supply of cattle for the packers. The stockyards and packers were interdependent, twins, joined at the hip.

The doomed cattle were driven by men on horseback away from the stockyard scales and across the bridges to the packing plants. A rusting bridge over the Kaw River remains standing today just west of the American Royal complex. - impassable but symbolic.

One of the packing plants was Plankington & Armour, which opened in 1870. The acknowledged father of the packing-house industry was Chicago's Phillip Danforth Armour. His brother, Simeon Brooks Armour, moved to Kansas City to co-found Plankington & Armour.

Simeon established a company no-smoking policy applicable to all employees except himself. The Saga of the Armour Family in Kansas City, 1870-1900, by Edwin D. Shutt.

In 1871, the Armours built a new plant near the junction of the Kaw and Missouri Rivers. Renamed the Armour Packing Company, the enterprise was immediately successful. It later became Armour & Company.

Armour was one of the first to make use of what had been packing house discards; it began using every part of slaughtered animals to produce soap, glue, fertilizer, neat's-foot oil, pharmaceuticals, and other derivatives ("every part but the squeal" as Phillip Armour famously said).

Soon others began to utilize the one-time waste. The Peet Brothers Soap Works was organized in 1872, to take advantage of the nearby packers' byproducts. It would merge with Palmolive to form Palmolive Peet Soap Company.

In 1881, Fowler Brothers Packing House was founded. It covered several acres near the Armour plant, and its specialty was the refining of lard.

Swift & Company opened a West Bottoms plant in 1887. An immigrant who found employment there was Jose Gaitan, who crossed the Rio Grande River at the age of fourteen and later became a naturalized citizen of the United States. Jose's son, Fernando Gaitan Sr., was an Armour employee and also served in the United States Army. A grandson, Fernando Gaitan Jr., is a distinguished member of the federal judiciary in Kansas City, a judge of the United States District Court for the Western District of Missouri.

Proctor & Gamble initiated its West Bottoms operation in 1903. The Cincinnati-based company became the world's largest soap maker. In 1933, its Oxydol soap powder sponsored a popular daytime radio show, and in time P & G began to produce as well as sponsor the radio shows. They came to be

Cattle Trails And West Bottom Tales

known as "soap operas." In the 1950s and 1960s, many of the first televised "'soaps" were sponsored and produced by P & G.

Armour was an important part of the West Bottoms community for its whistle.

> "Armour's plant had a big steam whistle and it was blown every night at 9 o'clock. People set their clocks and watches by the whistle. It was also 'curfew' for the kids and they knew that they had better be home by then or not far away (a far cry from today). This whistle also was used as a fire alarm in the packing house area. The number of blasts on the whistle indicated the part of the area the fire was in." The Kansas City Kansan, November 24, 1985.

The six-foot-long whistle was turned over to the City of Kansas City, Kansas by the salvage company that razed the packinghouse buildings in 1964 and 1965.

The Kansas Stockyards Company needed more packers for its livestock and to that end invested hundreds of thousands of dollars in luring other major slaughtering houses to Kansas City's West Bottoms. The success enjoyed by the Armour family was a further inducement.

The Armours were among Kansas City's most important and influential families for the next 30 years. They were bankers as well as meatpackers, and civic leaders and philanthropists.

Fowler Brothers Packing House Employees
Kansas City Star photo

C O W T O W N

Cattle Trails And West Bottom Tales

Plant of Armour Packing Co. Kansas City, U. S. A.

The Armour Packing Company plant near the Missouri – Kaw River junction
Mrs. S. J. Ray postcard collection, Missouri Valley Room
Kansas City, Missouri Public Library
Kansas City, Missouri

COWTOWN

Cattle Trails And West Bottom Tales

THE COWBOY

Thanks to Joseph McCoy's efforts, Abilene was the destination of great herds of wild Texas Longhorn cattle, driven up the Chisholm Trail by equally wild cowboys who found recreation in Abilene at the conclusion of their cattle drives. They were an assemblage of daredevils, for most of whom driving a herd of Longhorns across the plains provided more adventure than they had bargained for...one trip was enough.

> "There were veterans who had starved during the last days of Appomattox with Lee, second sons of English nobility, Negroes new to freedom, steamboat gamblers 'on the lam', overland freighters, farm boys running away from home, Mexican vaqueros, and half-breed comancheros." Cowboys; The End of the Trail; by Alton Pryor, supra.

In his Historical Sketches of Cattle Trails of the West and Southwest, published in 1877 by Ramsey, Millett & Hudson of Kansas City, Joseph McCoy described the payday capers of the cowboy, who entered the dance hall just as he dismounted from his cow pony, still wearing his sombrero, spurs and pistol...and sometimes coming to a bad end. An old cowboy song told the story briefly:

> "Once in the saddle I used to go dancing,
> Once in the saddle I used to go gay,
> First to the dram house and then to the card house,
> Got shot in the breast, I am dying today."

Another cowhand's epitaph was even more succinct: "Here lies Les Moore. Shot by a .44. No Les. No Moore." Cowboys: The End of the Trail; Alton Pryor, supra.

Some attributed the founding of Abilene to Divine Providence. But according to C. M. Pipkin, a market correspondent for the Kansas City Stockyards, it acted more like a child of Satan. In 1871, Abilene employed a gunslinger named Hickok as town marshal. He was paid $150 a month, plus 50 cents for every stray dog he shot. The new marshal's given name was William Butler, but he was better known as Wild Bill Hickok, for good reason.

A lawman with a formidable reputation as a gunfighter was needed to tame Abilene, and Wild Bill Hickok appeared to be just the man for the job. He didn't stay long. He kept order during the cattle season of 1871 but the following October he was too quick on the draw in an incident in which he killed two men. He was discharged by city officials. He later joined Buffalo Bill Cody and Texas Jack Omohundro in show business - a prudent career change since his marksmanship was beginning to suffer from glaucoma, a condition diagnosed by a Kansas City doctor.

COWTOWN

Cattle Trails And West Bottom Tales

"DANCE-HOUSE."

Missouri Valley Room Photo

1872

The citizens of Abilene determined to be rid of the causes of all the trouble — the cows and the cowboys. This was accomplished, and by the summer of 1882 Ellsworth, Kansas had replaced Abilene as the Chisholm Trail hot-spot. The Abilene Chronicle newspaper editorialized:

> "Business is not as brisk as it used to be during the cattle season, but the citizens have the satisfaction of knowing that hell is more than sixty miles away."

The Kansas City that Wild Bill visited for medical treatment was an improvement over Abilene, but cattlemen with money in their pockets still came looking for a good time. The shows at the Theater Comique near the city market at the corner of 4th and Walnut were attended by stockyards people and cowboy visitors, including Wild Bill, Buffalo Bill and Texas Jack occupying one of the sixteen private boxes, joined by show girls and swilling "red likker.'

Western illustrator Frederic Remington was half-owner of a Kansas City saloon and part-time artist when he began to consider seriously a career change. He was encouraged to become a professional artist by Kansas Citians' acceptance of his early work, which he bartered for essentials before he began to sketch and paint in earnest. An exhibit in the West Bottoms' American Royal Museum proclaims: "Kansas City was an inspiration to the great western artist Frederic Remington. He created his first works in Kansas City, recording the experiences, aspirations and adventures of the people of the west."

Remington's representation of cowboys as heroic contributed to the world's enduring love affair with them. Every kid wanted to be one.

C O W T O W N

Cattle Trails And West Bottom Tales

Remington sold one early painting to a friend and lit his cigar with the check, before leaving Kansas City to become a professional artist.

A Remington bronze, "The Bronco Buster", may be seen at Kansas City's Nelson – Atkins Museum of Art.

The cowboys who were "drovers" (a British term for livestock herding) were vagabonds on horseback according to Alton Pryor, supra.

Waylon Jennings cautioned in song: "Mammas Don't Let Your Babies Grow Up To Be Cowboys."

Texas Longhorns were disappearing, replaced by cattle from neighboring states, different breeds that did not need fattening.

The cowboy drover disappeared along with the Longhorns, and the invention of barbed wire ended the open range essential to trail drives, hastening their demise after twenty epic years.

Wild Bill Hickok (above right) joined Buffalo Bill Cody in show business.
They also hang together on the wall of the Golden Ox.
The Cowboys, Time-Life Books 1973, Time Inc.

C O W T O W N

Cattle Trails And West Bottom Tales

THE IRISH

Pat O'Neill's entertaining, informative "From the Bottom Up: The Story of the Irish in Kansas City"; Seat 0' The Pants Publishing, 2000 describes the establishment of Annunciation Parish by 30 Irish families in the West Bottoms in 1872. Their pastor, Father William J. Dalton, kept a watchful eye on his flock; O'Neill quotes the Kansas City Times: "In the rough and tumble days of the 'West Bottoms' he rode about nights on a pony, making his calls." The stockyards and packing houses offered employment to many Irish immigrants and within a decade Father Dalton had one of Missouri's largest Catholic congregations.' In 1873, Kansas City's first St. Patrick's Day Parade ended at Annunciation Church, where a new church bell was washed, anointed and blessed in celebration of the occasion.

Unidentified children standing outside Annunciation Parish hall
Missouri Valley Room Photo

According to O'Neill those Irish immigrants, upon their arrival in the West Bottoms, found in the words of a reporter, "A wild place filled with cowboys, gamblers, and desperate characters... and no decent place to live." The reporter continued:

> "Irish single men and families found temporary, if sordid, living quarters in ramshackle rooming houses in the flood plain. Some shared a neighborhood called 'Hell's Half Acre', a slum north of Ninth Street, with Negro laborers and their families"

C O W T O W N

Cattle Trails And West Bottom Tales

A Kansas City Times article reported that investigation of Alderman Kelly's West Bottoms well had led to the discovery of two dead rats at the bottom. "The water has had a peculiar taste for some time." From the Bottom Up.

Yard workers and managers and packing-house employees often lived beyond the giant bluff to the east, scaling it after work to go home for the night.

Many of the Irish moved south, out of the Bottoms to an area around Southwest Boulevard — still close to the stockyards and packing houses where they worked. There they formed the city's largest and most identifiable Irish neighborhood. From the Bottom Up, supra.

Earliest known photo of a Kansas City St. Patrick's Day Parade.
Kansas City Star Photo

C O W T O W N

Cattle Trails And West Bottom Tales

JAMES PENDERGAST

James Pendergast, an Irishman of Tipperary lineage, arrived in Kansas City in 1876 and went to work as a puddler at the A. J. Kelly Iron Foundry. "He found himself in the midst of an international convention of traders, speculators, prospectors, salesmen of gold bricks and snake oil, and sports." Tom's Town: Kansas City and the Pendergast Legend by William N. Reddig, 1947, University of Missouri Press.

The West Bottoms, in its hey-day, was the "wide-open, raw image of Kansas City. It was the symbol of Kansas City, as Kansas City symbolized the West." James B. Steele, Kansas City Star, September 18, 1967.

There were also a lot of gamblers. "Scholarly gamblers like 'Canada Bill', who kept himself solvent betting on Webster's spelling and definition of words, and colorful plungers like Wild Bill Hickok, the two-gun marshal of Abilene, Kansas, made the town their headquarters." Tom's Town, supra.

Gambling was conducted in high style by the professionals.

> "Bob Potee's Number Three Faro Bank was one of the most famous gambling halls west of the Mississippi, and the gambler, Mr. Potee, was riding high. There came a night, though, when a lucky citizen broke Potee's bank. Potee, dressed in ruffled shirt, cutaway coat and tails, and carrying a gold-headed cane, congratulated the winner, paid off, and strolled out of the hall, adjusting his top hat to a jaunty angle. After a brief stop at his hotel room, he walked down to the Missouri River...and kept on walking until his silk hat floated. They recovered his body downriver. In his room was the brief note he'd addressed to his fellow gambler, Charlie Bassett.

> "'Plant me decent', Potee had written. Bassett obliged, and, just as in the song, six tall gamblers carried Bob Potee's coffin to his grave." Kansas City: The Spirit, The People, The Promise by Patricia Ewing Pace; Windsor Publications Inc., 1987.

Jim Pendergast's life changed when he placed a winning bet on a race horse, a long shot named Climax, and with the proceeds set himself up as the proprietor of a hotel in the West Bottoms, the American House. The hotel's saloon he named Climax, after the horse.

Pat O'Neill wrote that saloonkeepers in the Irish community "sometimes became politicians by default. They were gregarious by nature and no-nonsense by necessity...Well-liked by his West Bottoms neighbors and patrons, Jim Pendergast was first urged to be a delegate to city conventions in 1884." From the Bottom Up, supra. And throughout the decade, the power and popularity of Jim the saloonkeeper grew.

Jim's saloon was just around the corner from Union Avenue, a short street that carried traffic to the train station. Climax was a reputable establishment, but Union Avenue was a different story.

C O W T O W N

Cattle Trails And West Bottom Tales

"Union Avenue society took a swashbuckling pride in a reputation for picturesque sordidness which was believed to compare favorably with the iniquity of New York's Bowery. Nothing was allowed to interfere with the business of making the transient's stopover at the midcontinent interchange point an interesting and instructive interval. At night the avenue leading from the depot became a midway blazing with light, tumultuous shouts of ballyhoo men and the cries of grays (the suckers of the day) being whisked out of sight. Booted cattlemen, silk-hatted gamblers, ticket scalpers, bunco artists, blanketed Indians, Kansas yokels, and scented ladies strolling by from Paris and New York, mingled in this boisterous democracy." Tom's Town, supra.

The entertainment activity in the neighborhood included the "wettest block in the world" on West 9th Street near the Missouri-Kansas state line...of the 24 buildings, 23 were saloons. From the Bottom Up. One of those in the liquor business on West 9th Street was Moritz Glass, a German immigrant who settled in the West Bottoms in the early 1880s. The Glass family lived at the same 9th Street address as their business. The area was not considered suitable for Moritz's teen-age daughter, Clara, who was sent to Baltimore to live with an uncle. Clara's grandson is Howard F. Sachs, a much admired Senior Judge, United States District Court, Western District of Missouri.

Pendergast catered to the men who worked in the packing plants and stockyards; his relationship with the Union Avenue crowd was entirely political – and effective. Within a few years he won recognition for delivering West Bottom votes for Democratic candidates. He also summoned his younger brother, Tom Pendergast, from the family home in St. Joseph, Missouri, to join him and get his own political career underway, finding a job for him at a nearby horse track.

Case Park, a modest tract at the edge of Lewis and Clark Point near the River Club, is the site of a statue of James Pendergast. He is there described as Alderman of Kansas City's First Ward from 1892 to 1911, the year of his death. A mustached Jim gazes down at the West Bottoms he once ruled.

The words on the back of the sculpture describe him as "fearless in his expression of his views", and conclude "Honored by the public he has faithfully served and mourned by friends whose loyalty he has earned."

COWTOWN

Cattle Trails And West Bottom Tales

The statue, a 1913 project of Tom Pendergast and other Democratic leaders, was originally a fountain designed by Fredrick C. Hibbard of Chicago. Placed in Mulkey Square at 13th and Madison in an area known as Irish Hill, it was neglected and vandalized. In 1990, it was renovated and relocated. The King of the First Ward now sits on "silk stocking ridge" as Quality Hill was known to the Bottoms folk. From the Bottom Up, supra. Appropriately, his back is turned to the nearby River Club.

He is flanked by a pair of seated children extending empty dishes. An inscription reads: "This monument erected by general contribution as a tribute to the rugged character and splendid achievements of a man whose private life were the embodiment of truth and courage."

Steve Noll Photo

COWTOWN

Cattle Trails And West Bottom Tales

William Clark and Meriwether Lewis, co-captains of President Thomas Jefferson's Corps of Discovery, scaled a projection of land in 1806 upon their return from the Pacific Northwest. Clark's Journal for September 15, 1806 notes "at 11 A.M. passed the entry of the Kanzas river…about a mile below we landed and Capt. Lewis and my Self ascended a hill…from the top of the hill you have a perfect Command of the river, this hill fronts the Kanzas and has a view of the Missouri a short distance above the river…" From Journals of the Lewis and Clark Expedition Online, copy courtesy of Dan C. D. Sturdevant Esq., Immediate Past President, Lewis and Clark Trail Heritage Foundation, Great Falls, Montana.

Jonathan Kemper commissioned the Corps of Discovery Monument by sculptor Eugene L. Daub (2000) that stands on Lewis and Clark Point today. From that vantage point the Shoshone Indian woman Sacagawea, Jean-Baptiste Charbonneau, Clark's slave York, and Lewis's dog Seaman overlook five counties and two states…well beyond the boundaries of Jim Pendergast's First Ward. The Foundation's Dan C.D. Sturdevant. confirms that the hill scaled by the co-captains was "undoubtedly the 8th and Jefferson hill" where the Daub monument stands.

Steve Noll Photo

25

COWTOWN

Cattle Trails And West Bottom Tales

Thomas Hart Benton, first United States Senator from Missouri (1821-1851) and staunch advocate of westward expansion, predicted that the small settlement at the junction of the Kaw and the Missouri rivers would be the future seat of a western empire. Today, "Frontier Kansas City", a mural painted by the Senator's great nephew, another Thomas Hart Benton, hangs in the River Club. Commissioned by a number of Club members, the painting depicts the view from Lewis & Clark's Point as it might have been in the early 19th century, and includes Indians, a mountain man, a sod buster, and westward emigrants.

Steve Noll Photos

COWTOWN

Cattle Trails And West Bottom Tales

BOSTON BRAHMANS AND BELFAST BUTCHERS

Charles Francis Adams of Boston, a Harvard overseer and descendant of American presidents, purchased a controlling interest in the Kansas Stockyards Company in 1875. He reorganized it as the Kansas City Stock Yards Company and assigned another cultivated Bostonian, Charles F. Morse, to manage the company. Morse found the city's bluffs and other steep inclines to be a challenge but, according to an undated issue of the Midwest Research Institute's Midcontinent Perspectives, he reported: "I like the bustle and stir of Kansas City. I think we shall like the place very well after getting used to the hills and holes." (Used with permission from MRIGlobal.) Morse boarded at the Coates House while he built his home on Quality Hill near Lewis and Clark Point.

****

Alexander (Alec) Renwick Eagle, a Scot from a family of Belfast, Ireland butchers (known there as "slaughtermen"), found work in the Kansas City packing plants. His first employer there was another Belfast expatriate, Thomas Bigger, who was one of the city's first packers and who slaughtered hogs for the English and Irish markets. In 1876, Alec went to work at Armour Meatpacking Company, employer of butchers of every kind known to the trade.

According to an Armour company history, it was the meat packers who first introduced the concept of the conveyor line, carrying animals past workmen assigned specific tasks for their dismemberment. Armour and Company (1867-1967); A Century of Public Service.

Alec Eagle was superintendent of the Armour hog department for 29 years. Anita Eagle Frevert, Ed. D., Eagle family historian, reports that Alec never lost his Scottish brogue and once won a silver loving cup in a Highland Fling dance contest. Alec was later joined at Armour by a younger brother John (Jack).

Alec and Jack Eagle were the vanguard of a remarkable family that would make many significant contributions to animal health and husbandry in the decades to come. Between them, Alec and Jack had eleven sons who worked in the packing houses, most of them on the Armour killing floor; one of them (Alec's son Robert) began there at the age of eleven. A third generation of Eagles also had Kansas City stockyard or veterinary medicine connections.

Hog butcher knife used by Thomas J. Eagle at Armour & Co.
Photo courtesy of Dr. Anita Eagle Frevert

COWTOWN

Cattle Trails And West Bottom Tales

Kansas City Star Photo

Before Henry Ford developed an automobile assembly line in Dearborn, Michigan, there was an animal dis-assembly line in the West Bottoms' Armour packing plant. Here the butchers like Alec Eagle repeatedly performed one or more steps on a semi-automated line, where hogs and cattle were killed, disemboweled and cut into parts.

C O W T O W N

Cattle Trails And West Bottom Tales

PROGRESS

Deere, Mansur & Co., the first branch house of John Deere's Moline, Illinois company, began distributing Deere's plows from 10th and Santa Fe in the West Bottoms in 1869; Kansas City would become the nation's largest farm implement distribution center. Now other important commercial establishments moved to the West Bottoms; Abernathy Brothers from Leavenworth built there a large furniture factory building.

By the mid-1870s, Kansas City was a complete livestock market, trading not only in cattle but also in hogs and sheep, horses and mules. The mule market was now one of the largest in the country; Guyton & Harrington, headquartered in Kansas City, was the biggest mule firm in America, with a 4,797 acre facility at Lathrop, Missouri. The state of Missouri would become the country's primary mule producer and the Missouri mule would be adopted as the state animal.

In 1876, another Exchange Building was built at 16th and State Line, on the Kansas side.

By 1877, with seven railroads operating out of Kansas City, its destiny as the rail hub of the Missouri Valley was assured.

****

Things were lively on the social front, as quoted by Doug Worgul in The Grand Barbecue, Star Books supra, citing the Kansas City Times." The city has been overrun by cow boys the past few days." August 20, 1878. "Crazy Alice was released from the county jail and is now skipping around the railroad yards in West Kansas once more." August 22, 1878.

Charles Gleed described the scene that year as follows:

> "The population of the city included as fine a collection of ruffian brotherhood and sisterhood of the Wild West as could well be imagined. Renegade Indians, demoralized soldiers, unreformed bushwhackers, and border ruffians, thieves, and thugs from anywhere, professional train robbers of home growth, and all kinds of wrecks from the Civil War." Charles Sumner Gleed Collection, Manuscripts Department, Kansas State Historical Society.

****

C O W T O W N

Cattle Trails And West Bottom Tales

Union Depot
Missouri Valley Room Photo

In 1878 a new train station opened on the Hannibal depot site — the Union Depot, a great French Renaissance structure with towers, cupolas and dormers. It was the second "union" depot in the country — only across the state of Missouri in St. Louis had railroads pooled their facilities in this manner. The Depot cost $300,000 with yards and tracks, and was called the "Jackson County Insane Asylum" by many who did not believe that so large a building would ever be needed. Kansas City Star, December 13, 1936. They were mistaken; even more space would be required.

****

George Newton Blossom came to Kansas City in 1878 and immediately assumed management of the dining rooms at the new Depot. A native New Yorker, Blossom had conducted a railway eating house and hotel in Brookfield, Missouri before moving to Kansas City.

COWTOWN

Cattle Trails And West Bottom Tales

THE LIVESTOCK COMMISSION MERCHANTS

The new exchange building completed in 1886 was substantial, three imposing stories of brick and stone. The Kansas City Star later (September 7, 1941) published a picture of this "mansion of a growing business" with its "roof grill of the fanciest architecture of those times" and wrote that "Within its elaborate walls many a fortune was born as the riches of the growing cattle country were being developed."

Entrance to Live Stock Exchange Building 1887
Photo Courtesy of Alan Rogers

"Among my favorite photos of the Exchange Building. Seen here in 1887 when it still sat entirely in Kansas and had been doubled from its original construction size of 1876. With its attractive stone trim, trees, fountains and fencing, it made for a pretty setting. If they could be identified, in this photo are, no doubt, some early Kansas City names."
Alan Rogers.

Many of the offices in the new Exchange Building came to be occupied by livestock commission merchants, critical to the evolution of the Kansas City market. The livestock trade required more services than railway employees or accompanying shippers could furnish, and O. James Hazlett described the resultant role of the commission merchant in the opening paragraph of "Cattle Marketing in the American Southwest."

COWTOWN

Cattle Trails And West Bottom Tales

"The Kansas City livestock commission merchant revolutionized the distribution of live animals in the American Southwest in the nineteenth century. The speed and volume in animal traffic fostered by the railroads forced entrepreneurs in the trade to seek new business methods...Utilizing the railroad and telegraph, the livestock commission merchant became the dominant middleman in cattle trade by the 1890s." Kansas History, a Journal of the Central Plains, supra.

Under the livestock commission system, a producer assigned his cattle to a commission firm at the stockyards. Prospective buyers then gathered in the alleys between the pens, sized up the cattle, made their picks, and bargained over prices with salesmen representing the sellers. The commission merchant took custody but did not take title to the cattle, and received his fee on consummation of the sale. As Joseph McCoy wrote:

"The business of the livestock commission merchants is to take care of, feed, water, sell and render to the owner an account of such consignments of livestock as he may be able to obtain either from his patrons direct or from such as may arrive with stock not consigned to any other house...They are as a class honest, fair businessmen. Indeed, they could not be otherwise and succeed for any considerable length of time, because the competition and rivalry is so great and competitors so watchful that any other than an upright, correct manner of doing business would be exposed and published to the world." Historical Sketches of the Cattle Trails of the West and Southwest, supra.

However, some commission firms employed solicitors and McCoy's description of these people was vastly different, and colorful. After praising the commission firms' efforts as "worthy of success and fraught with great good to western and southern livestock men as well as to Kansas City", he went on to say that "certain adjuncts or aids of some commission firms may be of interest to the general reader" and continued:

"Active men are employed to perform various duties; but the particular class now referred to are the solicitors — those whose duty it is to meet every train and secure such stock as has not been consigned to any commission house. So soon as an incoming train is announced as nearing the stock yards, the hurrying tramps of solicitors, vulgarly but not inappropriately called 'Scalpers', may be heard hustling toward the unloading platform. If there is a shipper on the train whose stock is not consigned, they proceed in a cheeky sang froid manner to interview him, presenting the business cards of the commission firms which have the Scalpers employed. Such oily persuasive arguments as scarce ever fell from a mortal's lips are poured into the ear of a newly arrived shipper."

In his history of the early years of the Kansas City stockyards, Cuthbert Powell wrote of McCoy:

"A familiar figure here was J. G. McCoy. He was among the first to encourage the Texas cattle business and was known by everyone in the trade from Kansas City to

C O W T O W N

Cattle Trails And West Bottom Tales

Texas. He was a builder of the stock yards at Abilene, Kansas, and established a shipping point there in 1869. He was a man of wonderful energy and perseverance, but the railroads were against him and finally through their duplicity and treachery he was ruined." Twenty Years of Kansas City's Live Stock and Traders, Cuthbert Powell, Pearl Printing Company, Kansas City, Missouri, 1893, from the library of John Dillingham.

The latter comment referred to a dispute with the Kansas Pacific Railway. The Railway had contracted with McCoy to place feed and bedding in its cattle cars but never paid him. Two years of expensive litigation were required for him to collect and meanwhile his fortune vanished.

McCoy left Abilene for Kansas City and entered the commission business but was unable to compete with the established firms. He died in obscurity on October 19, 1915 in a Kansas City rooming house at 1315 Broadway.

It is worthy of note that Powell describes McCoy as a "stock yards" (two words) builder, and similarly his book title refers to Kansas City's "Live Stock" trade. This was the accepted industry spelling for many years. In this book, the spelling occurs interchangeably, reflecting the then prevailing usage.

Shippers and buyers needed protection in an industry with its Scalpers, and where legitimate transactions were quick and based on nods or handshakes. In 1886, the commission men formalized their Livestock Exchange organization with bylaws governing business conduct, financial and bonding requirements, and providing other regulations. Their purpose:

> "To maintain a commercial exchange, not for pecuniary gain or profit, but to promote uniformity in the customs and usages of the members; to inculcate and enforce correct and high moral principles in the transactions of business; to inspire confidence in the methods and integrity of its members; to facilitate and provide for the speedy adjustment of business disputes; to acquire and disseminate valuable commercial and economic information; and generally to promote the welfare of the livestock market at the Kansas City stockyards." Fred H. Olander, Kansas City Star, February 12, 1936.

The Livestock Exchange greatly improved the moral tone of the livestock industry, and when the Packers & Stockyards Act later established a pattern for self-regulation by livestock interests it was based to a great extent on the bylaws of the Kansas City Livestock Exchange.

A. J. Gillespie was the first to open a commission house in the Kansas City stockyards — in 1869, before the yards had a name. In the final chapter of his book Cuthbert Powell lists "the men who made the livestock trade" and his list includes the following note: "Nutter Bros., who came here this year (1886), and were in the trade for a long time, are now (1893) out of business." The 1886-1887 Hoye's Kansas City Directory lists the Nutter Brothers as "livestock com. K.C. Stockyards" with James A. residing at 324 w. 13th and Natis M. at 1113 e. 15th. The Nutters had moved from West Virginia to Kansas City. James later told his grandson, mortgage banker James B. Nutter, that handshake transactions were a matter of course in his stockyard years, and honored without exception in his experience.

By 1893 there were 70 commission houses. That year the speaker at a Kansas City meeting of the National Livestock Exchange described the attributes required of a competent livestock commission merchant as "the intelligence of a college graduate, the brain of a banker, the shrewdness of a broker, the sagacity of a lawyer..." After reciting several other virtues, he concluded: "added to all these characteristics he must have the handshake of a politician and the smile of a woman." Kansas City Stockyards and Packing House Interests, published in 1899 by the Kansas City Stock Yards Company of Missouri.

The Livestock Exchange organization was followed by the Traders' Livestock Exchange, an unincorporated association of traders at the Kansas City stockyards. The preamble to its articles of association stated a purpose similar to that of the Livestock Exchange, to wit: "organizing and maintaining a business exchange, not for pecuniary profit or gain, but to promote and protect all interest connected with the buying and selling of livestock at the Kansas City stockyards.

Commission men in Kansas City Stockyards pen
Photo courtesy of James Runyan Jr.

COWTOWN

Cattle Trails And West Bottom Tales

OTHER EARLY BUSINESSES

George Blossom opened his own hotel, the Blossom House, in 1882, across Union Avenue from the Union Depot. In the ensuing years it became one of the best known hotels in the American West. Trail hands from Texas stopped there, as did Sooners on their way to Oklahoma Territory and settlers bound for Oregon. It was possible to hear tales about anything, ranging from Eastern fashions to bushwhackers and Indians.

Steve Noll Postcard Collection

The New Empire photo, March 1903

The Star reported that presidents Roosevelt (Theodore) and Harrison had spoken from a Blossom House balcony, and noted that "the most surprising part of it all was the fact that the lowest walks of life next door to a president or other notable never seemed to cause the slightest trouble." January 1, 1913.

C O W T O W N

Cattle Trails And West Bottom Tales

(Photographed by Thomson.)
CUTHBERT POWELL,
EDITOR LIVE STOCK RECORD AND FARMER, 1880-'86.

Twenty Years Photo

Cuthbert Powell's career as a Kansas City livestock reporter began in 1878 when he became editor of the *Price Current*, a livestock paper first published in 1874 as the Cattle Trail. In Twenty Years of Kansas City's Livestock Trade and Traders, supra, Powell maintained that nothing exercised a greater influence on the stockyards' growth than the livestock publications. He cited "their ever keeping before the public the manifold advantages of Kansas City as a livestock center and packing point, and furnishing full and reliable reports of the markets to their patrons in the country and thereby invaluable aid to the dealers and the yard management..." And they were inexpensive; the price for a subscription to The Kansas City Packer and National Produce Review with its "accurate and reliable reports on livestock, grain and produce": 50 cents a year.

The *Price Current* name was changed to the *Daily Live Stock Record*, which became the first daily paper in the stockyards and later renamed the *Daily Drovers Telegram* in 1886. That paper later relocated in a new building at 1505 Genesee. According to the Telegram's 50th anniversary edition (March 9, 1931): "The front half of the second floor is set apart sacred to the editorial department, the sanctum sanctorum, the Holy of Holies around a newspaper office." The building stands today, occupied by the Amigoni Urban Winery.

COWTOWN

Cattle Trails And West Bottom Tales

It was Jay Holcomb Neff who renamed the newspaper "Daily Drovers Telegram" after acquiring it. The University of Missouri's Neff Hall housing the School of Journalism is named after him. Jay Neff was Mayor of Kansas City, Missouri in 1904 and 1905. "As We See 'Em – Cartoons and Caricatures of Kansas Cityans by Vintage Kansas City"

JAY H. NEFF
Mayor of Kansas City.

****

Banking services were pioneer stockyards enterprises, replacing a cash and carry system. Banks in the stockyards handled deposits for ranchers' sales, and ranchers borrowed money at those same institutions. Now bigger trades could be made in half the time and at half the expense as before, when the trader had to drive into the country and carry cash with him. The Livestock Exchange Building completed in 1876 had two banking rooms.

The first banks were unsuccessful and quickly went out of business: "Without effective regulation, county banks specializing in extending credit to finance cattle and grain trading passed in and out of existence, with dizzying speed." At the River's Bend, supra. But they were followed by more conservative institutions that avoided liberal loans for wildcat and speculative schemes. A

37

Cattle Trails And West Bottom Tales

contemporary photo of the Exchange Building shows signs on an exterior wall for Bank of Kansas City and Stock Yards Bank. In 1881, these two stockyards banks merged to form the Kansas City Stock Yards Bank, which became a part of the Interstate National Bank organized by meatpacker Simeon Brooks Armour. There followed a branch of the National Bank of Commerce, later to become the Stock Yards National Bank.

Livestock Exchange Building, 1876
Twenty Years Photo

More hotels came to the West Bottoms. One of them, the Stockyards Hotel, had tile floors and a $1.60 per night room rate. There were others, including the Drovers and the St. Louis down the street on Genesee. They catered to cattlemen who were overnight patrons while their livestock business was transacted. They had ridden into town in a freight train's caboose, free of charge behind carloads of their cattle that they tended en route, and they would ride home in style after a day or two, in a passenger coach and using free passes from the railroad.

****

Arthur E. Stilwell's West Bottoms printing plant catered to the local packing houses before he went into the railroad business. He first ran trains into Kansas City in 1890 - the Kansas City Suburban Belt Railway served the riverside commercial and industrial districts of Kansas City. Later, Stilwell assembled a line going south, linking Kansas City to the Gulf of Mexico. Kansas City Spirit by Bruce Mathews, published by Kansas City Star Books. A Missouri railroad acquired by Stilwell was the Splitlog Line of Wyandot Indian Mathias Splitlog, for $50,000. Today's Kansas City Southern Railway Company resulted from a reorganization of Stilwell's railroad in 1900.

COWTOWN

Cattle Trails And West Bottom Tales

There was significant passenger train activity by railroads going other directions. A Union Pacific Railway ad boasted of "The only line leaving Kansas City after the Operas, Lodge Meetings and Sunday night Church services, at 10:45 p.m., and arriving in St. Louis at 7:20 a.m. in time for all Eastern connections." For those going west, the Frisco line "Crosses three Ranges of Mountains" and "Harvey Dining Halls are a fixture on the entire line." Kansas City Stock Yards and Packing House Interests, supra.

****

Columbian Steel Tank Company was organized in 1893 by Andrew Kramer. Kramer had attended the Chicago World's Fair: Columbian Exposition that year, marking the 400th anniversary of Columbus' landing in the New World. He named his new company for the Exposition. Like Christopher Columbus, the Columbian Steel Tank Company was a pioneer...in the manufacture of stock watering tanks and grain bins for the agriculture industry. The West Bottoms of Kansas City, home of the stockyards with its animals in the tens of thousands as well as its demand for large grain elevators, was an obvious choice for the manufacturing plant.

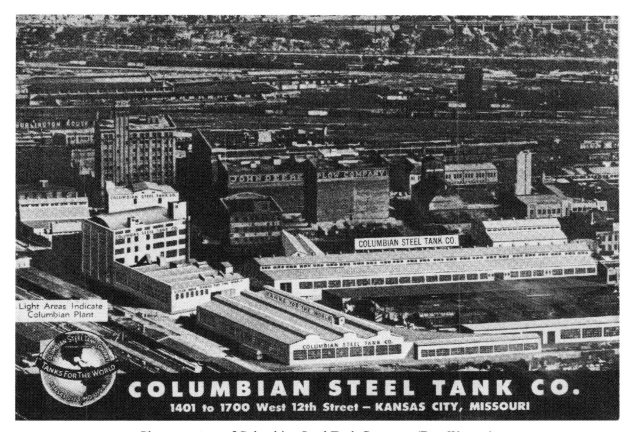

Photo courtesy of Columbian Steel Tank Company (Don Wagner)

COWTOWN

Cattle Trails And West Bottom Tales

FROM OXEN TO CABLE CARS

Before the Civil War (or "prior to the late unpleasantness" as Cuthbert Powell preferred to put it), horses, mules and even oxen were the usual mode of transportation: "It is still within not only the memory but experience of living and active dealers when oxen were counted among the legitimate holdings of a sales stable and teams of these faithful brutes were as regularly sold to freighters across the plains as horses and mules." Longhorn steers were broken for draft duty as well according to Powell, by yoking them in the middle between pairs of tame oxen, two oxen at the wheel and two in the lead. However, more and more cross-country shipping and transportation requirements needs were being satisfied by the railroads. "The laying of iron rails and the snorting of the iron horse" accompanied the march of progress and civilization across the plains. (Cuthbert Powell). The continued development of Kansas City and its livestock trade ensued.

In Kansas City, horse cars and mule cars had operated for many years but they provided a leisurely mode of transportation that was little better than walking. After the invention of the cable car, things changed. An enterprising young engineer named Robert Gillham, later a promoter of Kansas City, Missouri parks and boulevards (Gillham Road), was granted the franchise for a cable car system. Cable car movement was controlled by the grip, a device that gripped and released a constantly moving cable. The operator was called a gripman.

Cable Car
Kansas City Star Photo

In 1882, Gillham applied his engineering skills to the bluff that loomed over the West Bottoms traffic. He built a cable line on Eighth Street that started on Woodland Avenue, rounded "Dead Man's Curve" at Grand Avenue, and finished with a trestle at the end of Ninth Street that plunged a half mile from bluff-top to the Union Depot below, where a turntable reversed cars for the return trip.

An article in the Historic Kansas City Foundation's Possum Trot Gazette 1870-1890 described the maiden voyage. It noted that cable car mechanical failures were well known, and consequently "when

Cattle Trails And West Bottom Tales

the great day came when the cars were ready to make their fearsome descent the cars were filled with probably as nervous a group of outwardly brave men as ever assembled."

The "great day" was in 1885 and the trip down was described in the Gazette as follows:

> "The cars slowly approached the brink of the incline, they hesitated a moment, then began to pick up speed as they started downward. Here the courage of the intrepid explorers who filled the cars failed. One man ran to the door and jumped out and panic followed. Before the cars had had time to progress a few feet they were completely emptied except for the gripman and the conductor and they made their trip to the union depot in grand if empty splendor."

From the elevated cable station at the bottom, the dauntless twosome descended the steps to a waiting room on Union Avenue.

When nothing happened on subsequent trips, Kansas Citians cautiously began to adopt the cable cars. Railroad travelers were reluctant to try their luck, however, which was one reason for the success of George Blossom's establishment.

> "The big bluffs overlooking the old station and the near perpendicular Ninth Street cable incline were dangers that a great many travelers did not care to brave, especially with the Blossom House a nearby haven." Kansas City Star, January 1, 1915

The precipitous Ninth Street cable incline that tested the courage of travelers
Kansas City Star Photo

C O W T O W N

Cattle Trails And West Bottom Tales

The elevated terminal of the Ninth Street cable line in the West Bottoms
Missouri Valley Room Photo

The incorporators of the Metropolitan Street Railway Company included West Bottom meatpackers Simeon Armour and Andrew Watson Armour. When their company purchased the street railway system, the Fifth, Twelfth and Eighteenth Street horse car lines serving the West Bottoms were converted to cable lines. Kansas City was beginning to look like San Francisco.

By January 1, 1897, Kansas City had the best streetcar system in the world according to The Kings and Queens of the Range. Mrs. John H. Gregory was the editor and publisher of that work, "the only magazine published exclusively for the families of stockmen." Its office was in the Livestock Exchange Building, and the price of subscription was $1 per year.

The Eighth Street tunnel leading to Quality Hill opened a few years later.

> "Getting out of the West Bottoms to the Missouri side by streetcar took some doing. The limestone hills on the east side of the river basin were fairly high and steep. And it was on the tops of these ridges where much of downtown Kansas City, Missouri was built.

> "The streetcar would meander through the Bottoms down its main street. Then it would enter its own right-of-way, a slowly rising steel trestle that climbed straight toward the hills.

> "I remember watching through the open window as the trolley climbed higher and higher, swaying precariously from side to side as it always did, slowly making its way toward the summit. Ahead was the mouth of the tunnel leading into Quality Hill that

42

COWTOWN

Cattle Trails And West Bottom Tales

was constructed at the turn of the Century." Terminal Junction by Steven Dushan Milakov, publisher Joe Vaughn Associates, Prairie Village, Ks

The late Steven Milakov's father was a Serbian Orthodox Priest, living in Singapore when he wrote Terminal Junction. "Even though he lived and worked on the other side of the world, Milakov never lost touch with his Kansas roots." Joe H. Vaughn, past-President Native Sons of Kansas City, past Historian Wyandotte County Historical Society.

Entrance to 8th Street Tunnel
Missouri Valley Room Photo

Mule cars were little faster than walking. Cable cars were an improvement
Kansas City Star Photo

C O W T O W N

Cattle Trails And West Bottom Tales

RED WHEAT AND RED MEAT

Kansas City profited from the influx of Mennonites from Southern Russia seeking religious freedom and immunity from military service. They brought with them a strain of winter wheat called Turkey Red. The supply of wheat became dependable; grain receipts in Kansas City mushroomed. The prospects for a successful milling business improved substantially. In 1869, Dewar and Smith built the Diamond Mills at the corner of Santa Fe and 8th Streets, with side track connections to the various railroads. The Kansas City Board of Trade was organized that same year. At first primarily a civic organization boosting improvements such as better roads and fire protection, it was to become the world's busiest trading forum for hard red winter wheat.

Grain, first gathered in country elevators, was shipped to the West Bottoms for storage until transferred to mills to be ground into flour for bakers and other consumers. In 1871, investors erected a large grain elevator, and by 1876 there were three of them with another under construction. And the Board of Trade, no longer a rather quiet body, was reorganized and incorporated in May of that year. Kansas City Illustrated Review, Enterprise Publishing Company, May 1, 1886.

Other grain elevators came to the West Bottoms and more and larger flour mills — all taking advantage of the West Bottoms' central location and the presence of seven railroads. The Santa Fe Railroad set about filling its own elevators and others. To further this it recruited farmers in Europe, offering low railroad fares and farm land along-side its tracks.

Santa Fe Railroad Grain Elevators, 1939
Kansas City Star Photo

C O W T O W N

Cattle Trails And West Bottom Tales

Henry Sosland, from Lithuania, arrived in Kansas City in 1890. He was not a farmer but a miller; he had operated the family grist mill in the old country. Upon arrival here he became a peddler. By 1894, he was able to send for his wife and three sons: Morris, Samuel and Abe. The Soslands settled in a West Bottoms tenement at 925 Wyoming Street. Six more Sosland children were born in Kansas City: David, Benjamin, Sanders, Fannie Mae, Louis and Hymie. An early family treat was the exciting cable car ride on the Ninth Street incline.

The Sosland boys augmented the family income by selling newspapers, the first journalism experience for Sam, David and Sanders. (From Sosland Family sources).

A small booklet published by the Kansas City Stockyards in 1893 listed as the chief products of the territory wheat, corn and oats, as well as cattle, sheep and hogs. However, despite the progress in grain storage and milling, the stockyard and packing house interests were still easily identifiable as the primary components of Kansas City's commerce.

Kansas City Stockyards
Ray Postcard Collection

COWTOWN

Cattle Trails And West Bottom Tales

An Armour plant expansion made it the 2nd largest meat packing plant in the country. The Armour complex was comprised of sixty-three acres, with several various-sized buildings separated by streets and lanes. It would rank with Kansas City's Convention Hall as a source of local pride.

A postcard from the collection of Mrs. S. J. Ray in the Missouri Valley Room Special Collections, Kansas City, Missouri Public Library, depicts both the Kansas City, Missouri Convention Hall and the Kansas City, Kansas Armour Packing Company. The card is notable for its treatment of the two Kansas Cities as a single metropolitan entity.

****

William E Burnett gave up his butcher's job at Armour to open a small meat market in the West Bottoms. The Burnett family lived on the floor above the market, according to his granddaughter, Jean Aylward Dunn. Florence Burnett, Jean's aunt, was born there in 1892. From the Bottom Up, supra.

By 1896, meat packing was Kansas City's major industry with 7450 employees according to the Daily Drovers Telegram. The rapid growth of the livestock market had necessitated frequent additions to the Livestock Exchange Building, with wings and Ls extending across the state line into Missouri.

C O W T O W N

Cattle Trails And West Bottom Tales

The ambivalent location of the Livestock Exchange Building led to occasional excitement in the building lobby. The border between the two states, once a bloody Civil War battleground, was now just a line of colored tiles in the building. However, those tiles had more than historic significance.

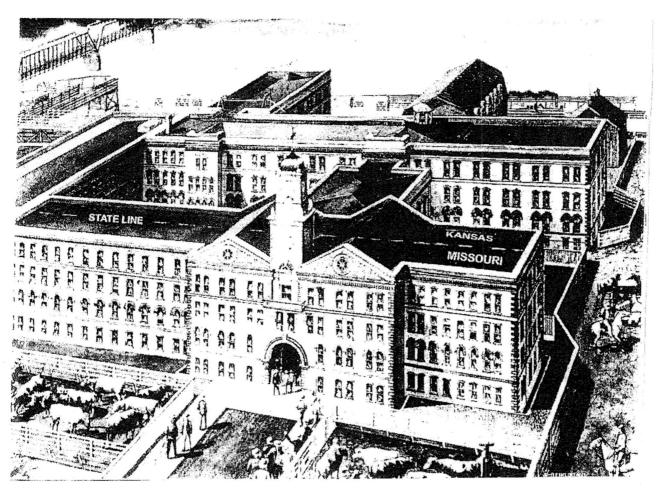

Drawing courtesy of Alan Rogers

"In the 1800s the exchange building straddled the state line. A class of villains known as Toad-a-Loops would escape arrest on the Missouri side by pelting into the exchange and making for its Kansas wing, where they were outside the jurisdiction of the pursuing police." At The River's Bend; An Illustrated History of Kansas City, by Sherry Lamb Schirmer and Richard D. McKenzie, Windsor Publications, Inc. and Jackson County Historical Society.

COWTOWN

Cattle Trails And West Bottom Tales

STRAWBERRY HILL

Strawberry Hill, one of Kansas City's best known ethnic communities, is an extension of the West Bottoms. "There was hardly a house there that didn't have a connection to the bottoms or the packing houses." Bernadette Soptick.

In the stockyards, unskilled workers handled the dirty work. They shoveled manure, hosed and repaired pens, forked hay and herded animals. Many of these workers were first generation immigrants. The same was true of their counterparts in the meat packing plants.

Bernadette Soptick is a volunteer at the Strawberry Hill Museum and Cultural Center at 4th and Ann in Kansas City, Kansas. Her grandparents were among those new immigrants. Her maternal grandfather came from Croatia and found work at Armour & Co. Once here, he married the girl next door, who was from Slovenia.

Bernadette's paternal grandfather, Mile Resovich, arrived in 1907 from a small village on the Croatian-Serbian border, and rented a room in the Bottoms. After quitting a packing house job that required clubbing sheep in the head, Mile Resovich went to work for a serum company where he was given the name "Mike Miller" on the company payroll. Then he sent for his wife-to-be.

> "When he left the old country, he told a family friend that, in time, when he had the money and their daughter was older, he would send for her to be his wife. In 1913 my paternal grandmother, Kata Bozich, set out for America to start a new life with her husband-to-be. It was a rough crossing in steerage with everyone seasick. She was told if you were sick you would not be allowed to enter the U.S., you would be sent back on the next boat. She was determined to make it to New York in good health, so she ate only oranges and stayed up top out on the deck.

> "After being processed through Ellis Island, she was put on a train with a tag on her clothing that said Kansas City, Kansas. Along the way different men tried to get her to get off the train and marry them in whatever city the train had stopped. She said no I am promised to another, and he paid my way.

> "It was a hard life being a new bride in the boarding house in the Bottoms." Bernadette Soptick.

Kansas City's thriving meat packing plants attracted unskilled peasants who signed on in the old country with the packers' European representatives. Once here, immigrants worked 14 to 16 hours a day, seven days a week, and were paid a nickel an hour.

The poorest packing house workers lived for a while in a shanty town in the Bottoms called the Patch, "a small piece of green grass and dirt and rutted roads sandwiched between the Armour and Fowler meatpacking plants on its East Side, and the curving Kaw River on to the west." For the Serbian population in particular it was home, "warts and all." Terminal Junction, by Steven Dushan Milakov, supra.

Images of Strawberry Hill, edited by Jennie A. Chen and published by the Kansas State Historical Society, features paintings by Marijana Grisnik who was born on Strawberry Hill. One of her images depicts a business section of the Patch, with the streetcar line to Missouri running down the center of the street. A caption notes that men from the Patch often carried buckets of beer over to the Armour Packing Company.

"The Patch" by Marijana, Strawberry Hill Painter

Patch houses were small huts made of boards, tin and scraps, without sanitation facilities or wells. Eight or more men lodged in each hut, and as men on day shifts left their beds the night shift climbed into them. Overview of the East European, Pan-Educational Educational Institute, by Sherry Lamb Schirmer, archives of Jackson County Historical Society ID66F2. Patch residents supplemented meager fare by fishing in the river, and retrieving beef livers from a sewer outlet below the Armour plant. Up From the Bottom, supra.

C O W T O W N

Cattle Trails And West Bottom Tales

There were also the railroads:

> "In my Dad's youth there were railroad tracks that ran down the middle of First Street. People would pick up coal and wood that would fall off the railroad cars to use for heating. Electricity was too expensive. They would pick up wheat and grain lying on the ground from the boxcars to feed their chickens." Bernadette Soptick.

Most of the Strawberry Hill Slavic population arrived around the turn of the 20th century and first settled in the Kaw River bottoms where they found work in packing houses, stockyards and railroads. Then they relocated.

> "As arrivals became more established and prosperous, they began to move up from the Bottoms onto the Hill. It became an ethnic enclave, a traditional village within a modern city, filled with Croation businesses patronized by Croation workers. Residents spoke the same language, sang the same songs, attended each other's weddings and funerals. As with all such communities, traditions continued to evolve with the passage of time and exposure to the broader American culture." Paul O'Boynick, M.D.

Dr. Paul O'Boynick grew up on Strawberry Hill. "The Hill was not singularly populated by Croatians. They were and still are at St. John's Catholic Church. Irish built St. Mary's Church one block west at 5th and Ann. Germans built St. Anthony's at 7th and Ann." Dr. O'Boynick's Holy Family Church dates back to 1908 when the original structure was erected by Slovenian immigrants – the parish is now well over 100 year old. There were also Polish and Serbian churches, and a Russian Orthodox Church was built at 6th and Lowell Avenue. Strawberry Hill was a wonderful community of profoundly Catholic and ethnic people, "where ethnic food and churches were abundant." Paul O'Boynick, M.D.

"The Bottoms could be a harsh and scary environment with men out of work, and the saloons and pool halls plentiful. But the hearty people persevered, and prayed in their churches to one day achieve the American dream." Bernadette Soptick.

Former Russian Orthodox Church, 6th Street and Lowell Avenue
Steve Noll Photo

COWTOWN

Cattle Trails And West Bottom Tales

There were also Indians. Mathias Splitlog was a Mohawk Indian who became a Wyandot following his marriage to a woman of that tribe. In 1852, Splitlog built a grist mill, the first in Kansas. The Wyandots purchased land at the fork of the Missouri and Kaw Rivers from the Delawares. After they petitioned for and received the rights of citizenship in 1855, the Wyandots distributed their tribal lands among the tribe. Splitlog thereby acquired valuable bottom land on the Kaw River, and more land on Strawberry Hill where he built a house. Kansas City Kansan, August 3, 1986. (Wyandot, originally "Wendat", came to be spelled Wyandotte.)

MATHIAS SPLITLOG RESIDENCE, 251 ORCHARD STREET, circa 1865/1885.
Photo courtesy of Wyandotte County Museum

Splitlog later sold his Strawberry Hill property to developers and his bottom land to the Union Pacific Railroad, and moved to central Missouri. He left behind a West Bottoms street that bears his name. The lucrative land sales gained international recognition for the millionaire Indian.

Alec Eagle and his wife Agnes also settled on Strawberry Hill. Captains Lewis and Clark had recorded that Kaw River water had "a very disagreeable taste." At the River's Bend; An Illustrated History of Kansas City, supra. Alec dug a well so Agnes would no longer have to carry home buckets of muddy Kaw River water. (Anita Eagle Frevert)

The Strawberry Hill Museum and Cultural Center at 4th and Ann on the Hill perpetuates the history and customs of the area. In the Museum are banners bearing the names of Saints. These beautifully crafted works of art were the standards of fraternal lodges established by residents of the Hill.

COWTOWN

Cattle Trails And West Bottom Tales

"When the immigrants were new to this country and working in the packing houses, they couldn't afford insurance. So they banded together and formed associations called lodges. Dues were collected, a low weekly fee, so in the event of their death their family would have money for burial purposes. These lodges served as a social outlet as well. There would be regular meetings, picnics, dances, ice cream socials etc. where they would be around people of their own nationality speaking their native language. A little taste of the homeland they missed so much.

"Most of these were nation-wide or fraternal societies, some connected to the local church. These lodges are still up and running to this day. Some have had to merge with others due to declining membership. I still belong to my Slovenian lodge, and receive its monthly newspaper which has a section written in Slovenian. Once when I was traveling in Ohio, my family and I dropped into a Sunday dinner being held at the local lodge hall. We had read about it in the lodge newspaper, and were in the neighborhood, so we figured why not. We were welcomed with open arms. What a warm feeling that was." Bernadette Soptick.

Lodge banners accompanied bridal couples in their walk down the church aisle and the caskets of lodge members at their funeral services.

Bernadette Soptick responded generously to a request for family history. She later wrote: "When I started seeing the journey of my ancestors written down, I felt it was my duty to give the best account I could. I am so proud and grateful to all of them. I just wanted to honor them in some way. Thank you for giving me the opportunity to share their story."

Kata Bozich Resovich, in her 1941 naturalization photo
Photo courtesy of Bernadette Soptik

COWTOWN

Cattle Trails And West Bottom Tales

FERDINAND THE BULL AND OTHER HAZARDS

Stockyard work was dangerous for the unwary. The case of Alexander vs. Crotchett et al, 233 Mo.App. 674, 124 SW 2d 534, was a lawsuit against the Kansas City Stock Yards Company and others by a man employed to drive cattle from stockyard pens to the various commission men to whom they were consigned. In this instance, when the plaintiff opened a pen gate to drive out the cattle, a bull lingered, and when the plaintiff tapped him on the nose with a heavy cane the bull charged him, causing injuries. This particular bull was unusually mean, a fact not communicated to the plaintiff. However, the case was decided in favor of the defendants because even an ordinary bull is dangerous and likely to attack on the very slightest provocation, and the plaintiff was aware of that characteristic.

The court cited as authority the saga of Ferdinand the Bull, from a children's book by Munro Leaf:

> "It is written that even the quiet and peace loving Ferdinand was distracted from his bovine contemplation of flowers, of which he was inordinately fond, and to which he was addicted, and aroused to a ferocious rage when he was unexpectedly stung in a susceptible spot by a bumble bee."

The court also noted that the Stockyards Company was required by federal statute to furnish its facilities to any and all shippers of livestock.

Another lawsuit against the stockyards involved a heifer instead of a bull. The heifer was wild, with dangerous propensities, but there was evidence that this fact had been communicated to the injured employee and the Kansas City Stockyards Company was exonerated.

Newspapers reported other lawsuits by stockyard employees for injuries inflicted by livestock, or by demolition work on abandoned pens, and the Kansas City Medical College recruited students by touting the educational opportunities afforded by the numerous railroad accidents.

Horses and riders fell on surfaces made slippery by manure and other substances, and untethered horses stampeded down stockyard alleys.

Blood on packing house floors wasn't always from slaughtered animals — accidents as well as occasional pay day knife fights contributed. Swift & Company saw 15 men killed between 1902 and 1910, and one Saturday at Armour an employee had his right hand cut open by a co-worker's cleaver and a carpenter fell into a vat of scalding water. Rise & Fall of a Cowtown, by Rick Montgomery, Kansas City Star Magazine, December 9, 2012. Upton Sinclair's classic novel "The Jungle", published in 1906, described the gruesome, dangerous tasks that packing plant workers were called upon to perform.

C O W T O W N

Cattle Trails And West Bottom Tales

Even recreation took its toll, with bare-knuckle fights staged in stockyard pens where hay bales provided seating for fans betting on favorites and buckets served as gongs to end rounds. Bouts were also staged in upstairs halls and even on sandbars along the river.

Politics had its rougher side too: "The devastating force of Tom Pendergast's fists and his ferocity when crossed were early impressed on the citizens of the river wards. His skill and daring in the manly art of self-defense did not diminish his popularity with the men of the West Bottoms..." Tom's Town, supra.

Not all fights were bare knuckled
"From the Bottom Up", Pat O'Neill

C O W T O W N

Cattle Trails And West Bottom Tales

FLOODS

The stockyards' location in the flat lands at the confluence of the Kaw and Missouri rivers was a mixed blessing — a transportation advantage, but flooding was a constant menace. On June 1, 1903, a huge flood swept the West Bottoms bluff to bluff. The stockyards were obliterated, thousands of workers and residents were evacuated, some lost their lives, and Jim Pendergast lived in his buggy directing rescue efforts and care for his constituents.

The flood forced the last Irish families out of the Bottoms, their neighborhoods destroyed. Florence Burnett, now 11 years old, was rescued from the rising waters by waders who deposited her safely on the back of a horse. From the Bottom Up, supra. William E Burnett relocated. Jean Aylward Dunn well remembers the new butcher shop at 5th and Main with sawdust on the floor and barrels of pickles. Florence lived to see the Burnett Meat Co. flourish once more, and to watch her son Bill McGonigle carry on the family tradition of purveying fine fresh meats in a McGonigle's market. She died at age 108, having given up cigarette smoking two years earlier. Jean Aylward Dunn.

The sturdy brick and stone structure of the Livestock Exchange Building was badly damaged by water that reached the second floor and rose to thirty feet in the yards; the entire building was later replaced.

In The Kansas City Spirit, supra, Bruce Mathews quotes Kansas City Star reporter Edward R. Schauffler:

> "Once upon a time, before there was any Union Station in Kansas City, the Missouri and Kaw rivers met one spring night in the waiting room of the old Union depot.

> "The rivers joined muddy paws and danced riotously in the waiting room where for twenty-five years passengers from East, West, North and South had assembled, to start, complete or interrupt journeys.

> "The passengers went away, to wait for nature to quiet down, and the rivers laughed, and whisked tickets out of filing cases, and covered them with mud, soaked suitcases and trunks, and drove locomotives to high ground."

The New Empire, a monthly publication with offices in Kansas City's Bryant Building (yearly subscription price 25 cents) published a Kansas City Flood edition in June, 1903. An introduction offered reassurance that "the people, undismayed, rallied to the work of repair and rebuilding even before the waters began to recede." The major structural loss in the West Bottoms was bridges. However, brick packing houses collapsed too - Swift & Company was one of the hardest hit with $100,000 in damages. The magazine also described "The Adventure of a Mule", a forlorn animal that stood on a warehouse step for three days in water to his knees, fed with corn from a box suspended near him. He was finally rescued by workmen.

Cattle Trails And West Bottom Tales

Among those displaced were Henry Sosland and his family. Rescued by boat from the 2nd floor of the building where they lived, they moved out of the West Bottoms. However, their journalism connections were by no means severed. In 1905, at the age of 16, Henry's son Sam went to work for the Daily Drovers Telegram as a copy boy. (From Sosland Family sources).

The 1903 flood also eradicated all but one of the bridges crossing the Kaw River. This led to construction of the reliable Intercity Viaduct. The first non-stop highway bridge to connect the twin cities, it opened in 1907, passing above the stockyards, packing houses and railroads of the West Bottoms. The bridge was later enlarged and renamed the Lewis and Clark Viaduct (1969).

Another flood occurred in 1908, relatively minor. The new viaduct was unscathed, proving it's worth. By this time, Armour & Company employed 5000 people in Kansas City. In 1910 it was still wet in the Armour plant. A September 23, 1910 letter in the archives of the Jackson County Historical Society (ID2505) contains the following: "The girls that work in the sausage department have to stand in water."

A tour through the Armour plant was enlightening. "They kill 3500 per day but I care less for canned goods since I have seen them working at it." Lulu Birely to Mary Ellen Birely of Keymar, Carroll County, Maryland.

Viewing the 1903 flood's devastation
Missouri Valley Room Photo

C O W T O W N

Cattle Trails And West Bottom Tales

View along Union Avenue in West Bottoms, showing Union Depot. (1903 flood)

The Intercity Viaduct traffic was not affected by the 1908 flood
Missouri Valley Room Photos

C O W T O W N

Cattle Trails And West Bottom Tales

THE SHIPLEY SADDLERY

The Charles P. Shipley Saddlery, established in the stockyards in 1888, relocated near the Stockyards Hotel in 1910 and was incorporated as Stockyard Harness Company. Shipley's new building housed manufacturing, storage, shipping and retail space, and a third floor foundry for the manufacture of spurs. A Shipley catalogue circa 1911, Catalogue No. 9, pictures the building and describes it as Charles Shipley's "crowning effort." (Kansas City Public Library, Missouri Valley Room).The catalogue offers evidence of the stockyards' nationwide reach:

> "In 1888 we established this business at the Kansas City Stock Yards and we have remained in the Stock Yards District ever since...We daily come in contact with and are personally acquainted with thousands of stockmen and farmers from all parts of the American Union — ranch owners and cowboys from Montana, sheep-raisers from New Mexico, orange-growers from California, and in fact all classes of men who are engaged in the various livestock and farming industries from the Atlantic seaboard to the Golden Gate are occasional visitors at the Kansas City Stock Yards."

The demand for Shipley saddles was worldwide, and notable customers included Franklin Roosevelt, Roy Rogers, Tom Mix, Gene Autry, and Will Rogers. (Will Rogers was part Cherokee and a tribal descendant of Jesse Chisholm.)

Gene Autrey's steers awaiting the packing house hammer

Tim Wigglesworth, owner of Naylor Serum Co. at 1625 Genesee, gave this photo of a small group of longhorn steers to Alan Rogers. "He told me they were shipped to Kansas City in late summer 1951, and were owned by Gene Autrey and had been featured in some of his Western shows." Alan Rogers.

Cattle Trails And West Bottom Tales

Shipley's aptly named Silver King had heavily engraved sterling silver on horn, fork and rear cantle, with a 10-carat gold horsehead mounted on the horn cap, and the entire saddle carried a wide border of silver ornaments.

CHAS. P. SHIPLEY SADDLERY
THE HOUSE OF FINE LEATHER

"SILVER KING"
Made to Our Specifications

There were also listed the Cherokee, the Little Wonder, the Cow Country, and the Candy Joe, among others. Number 60, Shipley's Famous Stock Yards Saddle, is described as very popular. The Shipley location, within a stone's throw of the stockyards, meant exposure to the working cowhands, most of whom rode Shipley saddles...high back saddles designed for them, with deeper seats and higher cantles offering greater support.

Shipley sold hats as well...including the Long Horn, the Tom Mix, and several John B. Stetson models. Every cowboy wore a hat, or sombrero.

COWTOWN

Cattle Trails And West Bottom Tales

Main Offices and Factory
Opposite Live Stock Exchange Building.

From
Factory
to Consumer
Direct.

From
Factory
to Consumer
Direct.

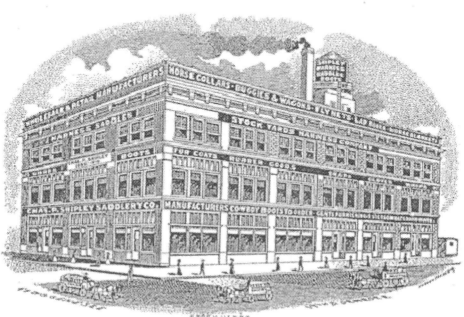

Write us for
any information
about Leather
Goods . . . .

Send for Our
Large, New Cata-
log of Saddles
and General Sup-
plies . . . .

Chas. P. Shipley Saddlery and Mercantile Co.

————— Wholesale and Retail Manufacturers of —————

Harness and Saddles, Boots and Shoes and All Kinds of Leather Goods

1527, 1529, 1531 Genesee Street,　　　　　　Kansas City, Mo.

Charles Shipley's merchandise had nationwide reach
Missouri Valley Room Catalogue

C O W T O W N

Cattle Trails And West Bottom Tales

Kansas City Stock Yards Livery Barn
George H. Lillie Photo from "Kansas City Stock Yards and Packing House Interests"
By The Kansas City Stock Yards Company of Missouri

COWTOWN

Cattle Trails And West Bottom Tales

MAJOR CHANGES

In 1911, a larger Livestock Exchange Building opened in a new location a block to the east, entirely within the state of Missouri. The capitol of the cowtown centered in the West Bottoms, it was the largest livestock exchange building in the world. It was also the last Kansas City investment by the Adams family of Boston. An earlier (November 12, 1910) article in the Kansas City Star described the anticipated 9-story building:

> "On the first floor are to be the shipping and receiving offices, a branch post office, telegraph offices, a foyer, cigar stand and barber shop. On the second floor are to be the general offices of the Kansas City Stock Yards Company and its banks. The seventh floor is to be occupied by the offices of the railroads, packing companies and the United States government." Article courtesy of Alan Rogers.

> The top (9th) floor would house the exchange's assembly hall and directors' rooms. There would also be the rooms of the Hoof and Horn Club. "This is a social organization, recently formed, and similar to the Saddle and Sirloin club of Chicago."

Exchange Hall
Photo from "Kansas City Stockyards and Packing House Interests",
Kansas City Stockyards of Missouri, publisher

COWTOWN

Cattle Trails And West Bottom Tales

The rest of the space in the building was to be occupied by the offices of the commission firms. There would no longer be iron or steel safes in the offices of the commission firms; each office suite was to be equipped with fire proof vaults so safes would not be necessary for the protection of books and documents.

A "For Sale" announcement in the Kansas City Star (January 1, 1911) offered building material from the old Exchange building scheduled to be razed on January 10. Included were window sills and stairways, three large building elevators, and bank fixtures. "Will load on wagons or cars if desired." Copy of announcement courtesy of Alan Rogers.

In 1912, Edward Morris bought the Adams group's 2/3 interest in the Kansas City Stock Yards Company and undertook a 6-year rebuilding program that included more railroad tracks.

Kansas City In Caricature, depicting people representative of Greater Kansas City, was published in 1912 by Howard G. Bartling. Its 288 pages reflect the business and professional life of the city at that time, much of it centered in the West Bottoms.

Thomas G. McCrosky, President Kansas City Live Stock Exchange	Frederick S. Doggett, Manager Blossom House

From the library of Steve Noll

COWTOWN

Cattle Trails And West Bottom Tales

UNION STATION

The frequent flooding was a major factor in the relocation of the railroad station. The Kansas City Terminal Railway was created after the 1908 flood swamped the Union Depot. The trunk railways serving the city – 12 of them, including the Kansas City Southern Railway and the Union Pacific Railroad – joined together to create and own the Kansas City Terminal Railway and build the new Union Station.

<table>
<tr>
<td>

W. J. Kinnear
President
Kansas City
Terminal Railway Company

</td>
<td>

</td>
<td>

From Kansas City
In Caricature

</td>
</tr>
</table>

The Union Depot closed in 1914, drastically changing the character of the Union Avenue neighborhood. According to William Reddig, "the building of Kansas City's present Union Station southeast of the Bottoms killed Union Avenue and threw a pall over the whole social life of the West Bottoms. The wake, held on Union Avenue on Halloween, 1914, was a carouse that inspired awed recollection for another twenty years..." Tom's Town, supra.

A Kansas City Star headline of January 1, 1915 read: "Blossom House is Dead." The article began:

> "Union Avenue, once the pride and again a thorn in the side of Kansas City, a street that resounded with the calls of the merchants' barkers and the high-hatted cabmen, lost its last hope of life at midnight last night when the Blossom House closed its doors as a hotel."

A view of the New Union Station as it appeared in 1915
Noll Postcard Collection

64

C O W T O W N

Cattle Trails And West Bottom Tales

FIRES!!!

A huge fire on October 16, 1917 destroyed more than half the stockyard area. The United States had declared war on Germany the previous April, and a New York Times article on October 17 reported that a German previously in the employ of the Kansas City Stockyards Company was suspected of complicity in a plot to burn the yards…"It is reported that the man was secretly removed from Oklahoma by government operatives." A subsequent Kansas City Times article, headlined "Arrest Six for Yards Fire", reported that men were being held in Kansas and Oklahoma in connection with the case. All were former Kansas City Stockyards Company employees and there was evidence of "seditious" remarks on their part.

A few days later an organization of Kansas City businessmen offered a $5000 reward for the conviction of the person who set fire to the stockyards. The organization's secretary stated: "We are certain someone deliberately set fire to the stockyards." And on November 18, 1917, a box maker described as a German was arrested and held for investigation in connection with the stockyards fire. It was anticipated that he would be turned over to government entities.

Men on horseback galloped through the flames to liberate trapped animals, but despite their efforts the fire killed a large number of cattle and hogs. A newspaper article at the time declared that the fire presented a challenge but "there is no fire or flood or any other calamity that can lick the men of Kansas City." The Hartford Fire Insurance Company covered much of the loss. A panoramic photograph taken at the time shows the charred remains of cattle and hogs, and smoke from the still-smoldering fire blanketing part of the yards. In one corner of the photograph is a draft for $1,733,779.99, followed by this Hartford caption:

> "Facsimile of draft for $1,733,779.99 given in full settlement of the fire loss and mix-up of livestock caused by the fire of October 16th, 1917, which destroyed twenty-five acres of pens of the Kansas City Stockyards Company. Twelve Thousand cattle and Forty-one Hundred hogs burned to death. Twenty-one Thousand cattle mixed so that individual ownership could not be determined. The promptness with which this tremendous loss was disposed of by the Hartford Fire Insurance Company places the Company in a class by itself with the Live Stock Interests of the country."

The yards were rebuilt, with brick-paved alleys and some pens floored with cypress for dryness. Despite their fire losses, Kansas City's horse and mule markets were able to provide thousands of head to the British government for the remainder of the war.

The stockyards fire was followed in April of the ensuing year by another, even greater, West Bottoms conflagration. This fire was in the industrial area 6 blocks north of the yards. It ruined about 3 blocks of buildings, completely destroying several, and doing $2 ½ million in damage.

C O W T O W N

Cattle Trails And West Bottom Tales

While the fire raged, two saloons at 10th and Mulberry continued to sell drinks until shut down by the fire chief. Kansas City Times April 5, 1918.

The Kansas City Times also reported (April 4, 1918) that no munitions were in any of the buildings where the fire originated and no war work was under way in the immediate vicinity of the conflagration.

As had been the case with the stockyards fire, this one was believed to have been incendiary in origin. However, a Times article the next day entitled "The Evidence Wiped Out" summarized the inconclusive end to the matter:

> "Although fire officials unite in the opinion that the big West Bottoms fire was of incendiary origin the cause will probably never be known. The complete collapse of the Abernathy Warehouse Building and destruction of the American Steel and Wire Plant have effectually erased all evidence."

Part of panoramic Hartford Fire Insurance Company Photo

C O W T O W N

Cattle Trails And West Bottom Tales

Fac-simile of draft for $1,733,799.99 given in full settlement of the fire loss and mix-up of live stock caused by the fire of October 16th, 1917, which destroyed twenty-five acres of pens of the Kansas City Stock Yards Company. Twelve Thousand cattle and Forty-one Hundred hogs burned to death. Twenty-one Thousand cattle mixed so that individual ownership could not be determined. The promptness with which this tremendous loss was disposed of by the Hartford Fire Insurance Company places the Company in a class by itself with the Live Stock Interests of the country.

Hartford Fire Insurance Company Photo.

COWTOWN

Cattle Trails And West Bottom Tales

THE AMERICAN ROYAL

Heather N. Paxton wrote the definitive history of the American Royal to celebrate its centennial in 1999. Underwritten by the Enid and Crosby Kemper Foundation, it is a Wallaroo book published by BkMk Press, University of Missouri-Kansas City in cooperation with the American Royal Association.

The American Royal began with a circus tent exhibition in 1899, following a series of annual shows by the Kansas City Fat Stock Show Association. The purpose of the fat stock show was to teach better methods of handling and feeding cattle for market. The first show, in 1883, resulted from a meeting the year before at Kansas City's Metropolitan Hotel (5th and May streets) of the city's "more enterprising breeders and feeders." Before adjourning the meeting, they unanimously resolved to hold a fat stock show the following year. Kansas City's Livestock Trade and Traders, Cuthbert Powell, supra.

Billed as the National Hereford Show, the 1899 circus tent exhibition was intended to increase awareness of the livestock industry, as well as of Kansas City. It also reflected the evolution of cattle from gaunt, durable Texas Longhorns to purebreds handled with the care extended to royalty. The "Royal" name was inspired by a Drovers Telegram editorial in 1901 entitled "Call it the American Royal" and noting a similar event in England called the Royal Show.

American Royal, 1902 version, held in this tent on Genesee between 17th and 18th streets. Three former shows had been similarly housed as well as several later ones.

American Royal, 1902, at 17th and Genesee
75 Years of Kansas City Livestock Market History,
Kansas City Stockyards Company

COWTOWN

Cattle Trails And West Bottom Tales

AMERICAN ROYAL LIVE STOCK SHOW, KANSAS CITY, KAS.
OCTOBER 9 TO OCTOBER 14, 1905

SWIFT & COMPANY PRIZE DRAFT TEAM

A 1905 American Royal Show was held in Kansas City, Kansas
Ray Postcard Collection

Heather Paxton chronicled various early-year Royal events held at several locations.

> "As the show grew, it became more difficult to find space to accommodate it. In 1908, a one-story stucco building was erected by the Kansas City Stock Yards Company at 20th and Genesee Streets. This arena, where the judging of livestock took place in the daytime and horse shows were held at night, was called the American Royal."

However, the Royal remained transient until 1921.

1921 saw the construction of the American Royal building at 23rd and Wyoming, a modern structure finished in time for the Royal activities in the fall of 1922. The Kansas City Stock Yards Company provided the land and most of the financing, with an assist from the American Shorthorn Cattle Breeders' Association, the American Hereford Cattle Breeders' Association, and the Chambers of Commerce of both Kansas Cities. The building was long overdue. John Dillingham told attendees at the October 21, 1999 Charles N Kimball Lecture: "In the beginning the American Royal adopted Kansas City as its home and remained loyal to the city through many tribulations. It got bigger every year, and yet it was the last of the big stock shows to have a permanent and adequate home." It's All About Eating: Kansas City's History and Opportunity. The building was destroyed by fire on Valentine's Day, 1925, but rebuilt in time for the American Royal events that year. It would serve until 1992, when the American Royal complex was built across from the Kemper Arena.

C O W T O W N

Cattle Trails And West Bottom Tales

AMERICAN ROYAL BLDG., KANSAS CITY, MO.—28

American Royal Building
Ray postcard collection

The first American Royal Parade was in 1926, and Will Rogers attended that year's horse show. Also that year, and the next, vocational agricultural students participated in the Royal's livestock judging contests. Then in 1928, a group of students from 18 states met at the Baltimore Hotel in Kansas City during the American Royal and formed the Future Farmers of America (the FFA). The 4-H Clubs (Head, Heart, Hands, Health), extensions of land grant colleges such as the University of Missouri and Kansas State to teach rural kids agricultural skills, also became part of the Royal, with participation in livestock judging competition - an important feature of every Royal. Many of the stockyard cattle traders served as contest judges; they had been judging cattle for a living all of their adult lives.

C O W T O W N

Cattle Trails And West Bottom Tales

American Royal Arena
Ray postcard collection

In the dismal Depression years, the Royal attracted record-breaking crowds. The American Royal president declared that the attendance was the answer of Main Street to Wall Street...short on cash but long on courage.

COWTOWN

Cattle Trails And West Bottom Tales

SOSLAND PUBLISHING COMPANY

Sam Sosland progressed from copy boy at the Daily Drovers Telegraph to free-lance journalism. He began writing reports on the cattle and grain markets and encouraged his younger brothers David and Sanders to become agriculture reporters. David became a cub reporter at Swift & Company's Kansas City Packer, and wrote copy and sold advertising for the Milling and Grain News in St. Louis. Sanders went to work with Sam in free-lance reporting; both were listed in the 1920 Census as newspaper reporters.

The three brothers, with help from their father, created the Southwestern Miller. The first issue of the weekly magazine appeared on March 17, 1922. The premier edition made it clear that in addition to providing news and market reports, the magazine would promote flour milled from hard, red winter wheat. This was the beginning of the Sosland Publishing Company, devoted to agribusiness and in particular to the milling and baking industries. (From Sosland Family sources).

David, Sanders and Samuel Sosland Circa 1922
The founders of the Southwestern Miller
Photo Courtesy Sosland Family Sources

Today, Sosland Publishing and its Southwestern Miller flourish. Milling historian Herman Steen praised it as an exemplary family enterprise:

72

Cattle Trails And West Bottom Tales

"The Southwestern Miller occupies a unique place in the conduct of one of the most basic endeavors of mankind. And inevitably associated with the rise to significance of this periodical is the tale of a family — a tale of unified trust and effort that in one generation carried its members from direst poverty to posts of leadership and honor and achievement. Such things are the essence of America." Herman Steen, 1969 (quotation provided by Sosland Family sources).

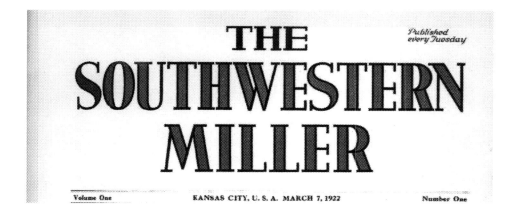

Cover of first edition, Southwestern Miller, June 1922
Photo courtesy of Sosland Family Sources

Emil Ruff had been known as the Bread King because his bakery at 9th and Hickory kept the West Bottoms well supplied with that staple; when he died in 1900 he left an estate of $50,000. Kansas City Star, September 28, 1967. Commercial baking companies later facilitated a general flight away from home baking, dramatically changing the flour milling industry and the production of bread and other baked goods. The abundance of flour led to the establishment of large commercial bakeries. The

Cattle Trails And West Bottom Tales

national chain Campbell Taggart Associated Bakeries got its start through the purchase of Kansas City's Manor Baking Company, As late as 1939, Manor's bread wagons were horse-drawn vehicles. Developments such as these made the Soslands' home town a unique setting for their publications about the milling and baking industries. Sosland Family Sources.

Ray postcard collection

Biscuit baking companies with their cookies and crackers found a home in the West Bottoms, including the Sunshine Biscuits of the Loose-Wiles Biscuit Company. This was the company of John L. Loose and his brother Jacob (Loose Park).

C O W T O W N

Cattle Trails And West Bottom Tales

STOCKYARD ACTIVITY

In 1934, the great horseman Tom Bass died. A former slave, he was the only African-American ever to exhibit at the American Royal. His waltzing mare, Miss Rex, was a crowd pleaser. Bass had trained thousands of horses, and his well-mannered mounts were indispensable in the stockyards. Stockyard regulars often disdained dismounting to perform their tasks and one characteristic of their mounts was the ability to stand in positions that enabled riders, without leaving the saddle, to unlatch the big hooks on the cattle pen gates.

Cattlemen had garage space for their cars in an old mule barn, as well as a stable for a horse or two. Daily they would park their cars, often change clothes in Orrin Haggard's Locker Room, mount their horses, and ride to work. It was a ritual.

Horsemen paraded down cobblestoned Genesee Street - sometimes even encroaching on the brick sidewalk in front of the Livestock Exchange Building - and on into the pens and alleys of the yards. The horses had a "yard gait", a fast walk so smooth that the riders seemed to float along, their Stetson hats staying level as they rode. Riders carried a whip or a cane, used to point to particular animals when they reached the pens. They would crack the whip and the sound would move the cattle around the pen, giving a buyer a better look before making a purchase. A poke with the whip or cane served the same purpose.

James Runyan Sr. sorting cattle - Owner seated on the fence, observing
Photo by HyLite Inc., courtesy of James Runyan Jr.

75

COWTOWN

Cattle Trails And West Bottom Tales

The stockyards in Kansas City were first designed for rail consignments as the iron horse replaced the cow horse, but truck shipments grew with highway expansion, serving smaller individual livestock holdings. In 1935, the ICC was empowered to regulate truckers engaged in interstate commerce. Many Missouri and Kansas truckers were not authorized by the ICC to engage in interstate commerce and could not cross state lines. However, because of its location straddling the border, the stockyards company could arrange its docks to enable Kansas truckers to unload in Kansas and Missouri truckers to unload on the Missouri side. So, while Kansas City with its excellent railroad facilities continued to do well in the long-haul business, nearby stockmen and farmers could take advantage of the trucking facilities. And the ability to readily move livestock from one state to the other offered timely opportunities to escape property tax assessments.

A June 2, 1970 Kansas City Star story prepared by Bill Marshall, head of the United States Agriculture Department's consumer and marketing office in Kansas City, eloquently described the changes over the years:

> "Old time cattlemen say that if you sit alone on the top of the old cattle pens in Kansas City and listen with your heart, you can hear the crack of the bull whip that urged the great trail herds of longhorn cattle which came to market a century ago.

> "And they say if you try hard you can hear the rhythmic clanking of the giant drive wheels – and even smell the acrid fumes of the shuddering smokestacks – of the railroad's 'iron horse' as it snaked out into cattle country to replace the 'cow horse' in pushing beef to market.

> "But if you listen only with your ears you will hear the whirring tires of the huge cattle trucks and the piercing blasts of air horns – the modern sounds of Kansas City stockyards…"

COWTOWN

Cattle Trails And West Bottom Tales

****

Texas fever was a disease caused by ticks carried north by Texas Longhorns on trial drives. The Longhorns had developed resistance to the disease, but it caused northern cattle to sicken and die when they came into contact with it. A Kansas law made it illegal to drive Texas cattle to Abilene, and the Chisholm Trail was closed for good. The Kansas City Livestock Exchange was influential in isolating the Texas Longhorns during this period, and quarantine yards were established on the west side of the Kaw River in 1886. A dipping solution of arsenic finally led to the eradication of Texas fever but not until the cattle drive was a thing of the past. The need for quarantine facilities ended when the federal government prohibited shipment of tick-infested cattle in interstate commerce. The yards, renamed the West Side Feed Yards, were then utilized to put livestock in the pink of condition for sale after long train journeys.

The closing of the Chisholm Trail did not mean the end of the excitement. In his eloquent memoir "The Stockyard Shaman", renowned sculptor and writer Robert Morris remembers the stockyards at their zenith.

> "The Kansas City of my preteen youth was divided into two quite distinct realms, two life spaces. One was more continuous, often grayed-out by stretches of school's tedium and the endless coping, the scheming and mini-dramas of family life. Then there were the stockyards...1 can remember the blazing summers when the acres of gates and chutes and sheds and scale houses stretched to the Kaw River and the noise of thousands of animals from the West, the slamming of switching freight cars from the East and the clanging of metal coming north from the Columbian Steel Tank Company, all combined in an indescribable cacophony that echoed off the bluffs that towered over the West Bottoms. I remember seeing crazed Brahma bulls rip 8-by-8 gateposts out of bricks as if they were matchsticks, and seeing 200 head of longhorns running wild-eyed across an elevated chute, and learning that until they were loaded onto a train in West Texas, they had never seen a man."

Morris is a native Kansas Citian, born February 9, 1931. He studied art at the Kansas City Art Institute and the University of Kansas, and has created many important works of art including the Glass Labyrinth on the south lawn of Kansas City's Nelson Atkins Museum and the stockyards' Bull Wall. Robert Morris's father was a livestock man.

COWTOWN

Cattle Trails And West Bottom Tales

Robert Morris inside his Glass Labyrinth
Photo by Toni Wood / The Nelson-Atkins Museum of Art

COWTOWN

Cattle Trails And West Bottom Tales

James Runyan Jr.in his Swift & Henry office
Photo courtesy of James Runyan Jr.

Jim Runyan had similar memories, of Texas cattle arriving at the Kansas City Stockyards, and their unloading: "Out of the rail cars they would come, fire in their eyes, they would jump fences, clearing all the alleys. They were big red, horned cattle."

C O W T O W N

Cattle Trails And West Bottom Tales

THE PLATTS

Mortimer R. Platt hailed from upstate New York. After practicing law there for a few years he became a gold and silver prospector in Idaho, a hay farmer in California and a mail contractor in Arizona. While in the postal service he carried mail from Tucson to Los Angeles. It was a distance of 500 miles through Apache country. According to family lore, he traveled only at night – the Apaches avoided night fighting because if they were killed after dark their spirit would not go to the "happy hunting ground."

In 1871, Mortimer came to Kansas City and entered the cattle and saddle horse business. When the Mastin Bank opened a branch in the stockyards in 1873 he became its manager. The only other bank in the yards, the First National Bank, failed shortly afterward and the Mastin Bank succeeded to all of the banking business in the stockyards.

Mortimer R. Platt
Twenty Years photo

The Mastin Bank later closed its doors but by this time Mortimer Platt had turned his attention to farming just outside of town. Mortimer bought two square miles of farm land in Johnson County, Kansas. Today much of Mortimer's farm is in the City of Leawood, between 83rd and 95th streets.

Cattle Trails And West Bottom Tales

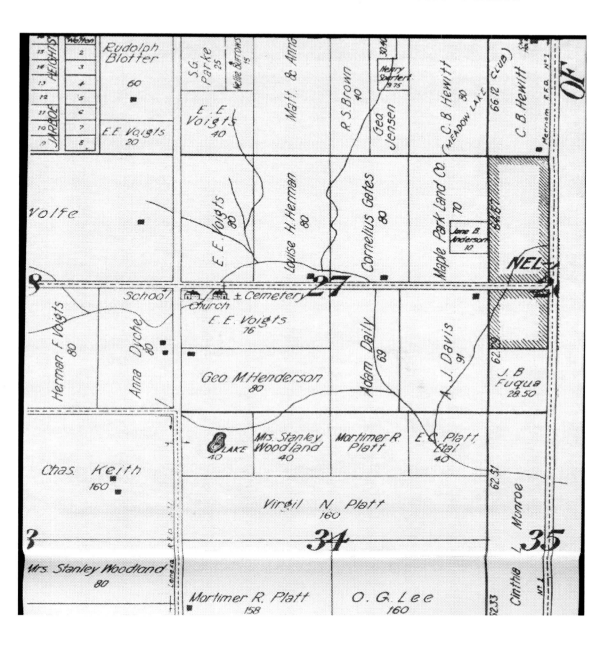

An old map of the City of Leawood, Kansas is reproduced inside the front cover of "Leawood: A Portrait in Time", by Ann Morris, published by the Leawood Historic Commission in 1997. Designated on the map are some of the tracts of land owned by Platts.
Courtesy of the Leawood Historic Commission, Janine E. Joslin, Chair

In 1875, Mortimer entered the livestock commission business. He maintained an office on Genesee Street across from the Livestock Exchange Building. In 1882 he withdrew from the trade in the stockyards and turned his attention to importing and breeding Galloway cattle. According to "Twenty

COWTOWN

Cattle Trails And West Bottom Tales

Years of Kansas City's Live Stock Trade and Traders" by Cuthbert Powell, supra, from a small beginning he built the largest recorded herd of Galloways in the world.

Mortimer was one of those enterprising breeders and feeders who founded the Kansas City Fat Stock Show Association in 1882, and he showed his Galloways successfully at the fat stock shows that followed - the forebears of the American Royal.

Mortimer Platt's brother Roy settled on a ranch in Comanche County, Oklahoma, where he too engaged in breeding and raising Galloway cattle. When Roy's cattle were ready to market he drove them to Mortimer's Kansas farm for fattening and then to the Kansas City stockyards for sale. Mortimer sold his cattle there too.

Mortimer Platt later built a Colonial Revival-style house at 3525 Harrison Boulevard in Kansas City Missouri's Historic Hyde Park District. Hyde Park District land originally comprised the city's first private country club, the Kenwood Golf Links in Westport, and before annexation by Kansas City the Westport City Council responded to club members' complaints over cows on the golf greens by passing a herd law prohibiting it. The club was relocated in 1896 in Seth Ward's east pasture, in what is now Kansas City's Loose Park.

Mortimer and his wife Beverly had five sons, all boys. No namesake for Grandmother Platt. When there occurred another shortage of girls in the next generation the youngest of the five sons, Ernest, named his son Beverly. This Beverly (Bev to his many friends) was the source of most of the Platt family information herein.

One block east of Genesee in the West Bottoms is the Fred Platt Horse Barn; the whitewash sign has long since faded away but Bev Platt can point out that barn where his older cousin Fred stabled his string of saddle horses. Most of the well-behaved Platt horses were leased to the cattlemen who worked all over the sprawling stockyard acreage and needed mounts to carry on their work.

Fred Platt bought his saddle horses from breeders in the area, and Bev sometimes accompanied him. Horses not leased were shipped to Eastern purchasers. The standard price to them was Fred's original purchase price plus his fee. Fred's purchases were the typical verbal, cash transactions, and Bev recalls asking his cousin how the Eastern purchasers could verify the price he had paid. Fred gave a familiar response: they took his word for it because in the livestock trade "a man's word was his bond."

COWTOWN

Cattle Trails And West Bottom Tales

KANEY'S KID

Another one with memories was known as "Kaney's Kid" around the stockyards. Everyone knew her father, Cliff Kaney. Today, she is Sally Kaney Tourtellot Ruddy, but in so many important respects she is still Kaney's Kid, with fond and indelible recollections of the stockyards and its people and its yarns.

Clifton John Kaney went to work for the Morris Packing Firm as an office boy when he was sixteen years old. After watching him "in harness" for several years, Evans – Snider – Buell Co. hired him as a butcher cattle salesman, a promotion. In 1919 he was employed by Swift & Henry, then officing on the first floor of the Livestock Exchange Building. Swift & Henry was formed in 1909 when James C. Swift, former law partner of future Missouri governor William M. Hadley, joined commission merchant Charles D. Henry. This was the genesis of one of the country's largest and most durable livestock commission firms. .

JAMES C. SWIFT,
President Swift & Henry Live Stock Company.
As We See 'Em – Cartoons and Caricatures of Kansas Cityans

C O W T O W N

Cattle Trails And West Bottom Tales

Kaney became Swift & Henry's president and owner in 1937, succeeding James C. Swift. Those were lean years and in Swift's final December 31, 1936 letter to customers, he offered assurance that better times were coming. James L. Runyan Jr., today the owner of Swift & Henry, tells how Kaney acquired the company:

> "In the mid-thirties, I think 1937, Swift & Henry suffered some huge financial losses. The bank took over the company. They offered the company to Mr. Kaney if he would pay interest on the balance and make monthly payments. After half the day haggling over the terms, Mr. Kaney told them he would pay off the actual loss, no interest, on his schedule out of company earnings. 'No way', the bankers said at about noon. Mr. Kaney said he was going over to the West End for lunch, and when he returned 'the company is either mine or yours'. He returned and, before he could get seated, they said 'the company is yours.'"

Cliff Kaney's job for many years was buying and selling cattle on commission. He visited ranchers and farmers throughout the Southwest, looking over herds in pastures and talking to ranchers about their markets and problems.

Sally went with Cliff on some of his trips, to Kansas, Oklahoma, Texas, and even New Mexico, as he looked at cattle on farms and big ranches. They would usually leave home on a Friday morning and return late on Sunday night. (Cliff needed to be on his horse and at work in the pens at the stockyards early Monday morning when the market opened).

> "Cliffy, my Dad, took me out of school when I was in Bryant to go with him on cattle buying trips. Mother protested, but we won. I met some colorful people and learned some colorful language. Cliffy told mother that when I got to be her age I wouldn't remember a damn thing about what I did that day at school, but I'd always remember what I did on those trips. And I do." Sally Ruddy.

Sally's recollections of those trips with "Cliffy" afford a good description of the activities of commission men away from the confines of the stockyards.

COWTOWN

Cattle Trails And West Bottom Tales

Clifton John Kaney and his kid Sally
Photo courtesy of Sally Ruddy

Jim Runyan Jr. finds it difficult to believe that Sally called the formidable Mr. Kaney "Cliffy." "He scared me to death."

Upon the arrival of Cliff and Sally at a customer's ranch, the rancher would take them to look at the cattle grazing in his pasture and point out those to be shipped to market. Then his men would arrive on horseback to drive the cattle to a corral near the railroad tracks.

> "One time the owner was short one man for the round up to the corral. Cliffy told the boss: 'My kid can help. The horse knows what to do. All she has to do is stay on, and she can do that.' So I did and it was great fun." Sally Ruddy.

COWTOWN

Cattle Trails And West Bottom Tales

At the railroad corral, Cliff would walk through the cattle in the pens, sorting them into groups of three for shipment — stockers, feeders and canners. Stockers were 400 pounders, sold for further feeding in a pasture; the feeders were big 700 pounders sold for finishing at feed lots. The canners were the runts, sold for canned meat, hot dogs, etc. After sorting the cattle were loaded onto box cars for shipment to Swift & Henry in Kansas City.

Sally waited in the car during these proceedings. The trips were in the Depression years...hard times that made a lasting impression on Sally. Cliff prepared her for what she would see as she sat there.

> "Now when the train stops a lot of men will jump down out of the box cars. They will walk past the car and look at you...maybe smile and nod. Don't be afraid, they are just men like me except that they don't have a job. They are looking for work. You may remind them of their own little girl they left at home. They hope to find work as a hired hand on a farm even though they may never have done hard labor."

It happened as Cliff predicted.

> "One thing I remember about the out of work men pouring out of the box cars during those Depression years is how they were dressed. In most cases they wore fedora hats and a shirt and tie under a suit coat with matching pants. They didn't own bib overalls or any other old work clothes. This was before the days of lounge wear and these were city men. They didn't trade at feed and tractor supply stores where customers were given caps to wear advertising John Deere, Purina Chow, and Staley Mash. The Mash was chicken feed, and one sign I remember in the Old Mill in Lee's Summit, Missouri: `If Staley's chicken feed don't make 'ern lay, they're roosters.'" Sally Ruddy.

Occasionally, Sally and Cliff would go to the farm home of the man selling his cattle and meet his family. In many of the homes the kitchen window had a wooden shelf fastened to the sill, and food was left on that shelf with a sign that read "help yourself".

There were also trips to Pawnee, Oklahoma. There a Pawnee Indian sat on a blanket outside the small cafe where Sally and Cliff customarily ate lunch.

> "He was making beautiful beaded moccasins. Everyone in town seemed to know and respect Pawnee Bill. I called him 'Mr. Bill' and Cliffy introduced me: 'This is my kid, Sally'. Pawnee Bill lifted his beat up old Stetson hat and said 'Miss Sally'. Cliffy gave me time to watch Mr. Bill work and let him draw around my bare feet for a moccasin pattern. It was a long time before Cliffy went back to Pawnee, Oklahoma, but when he did he returned with a package for me. He had seen Pawnee Bill and picked up my beaded moccasins. A perfect fit and perfectly beautiful. They were almost worn out before I outgrew them." Sally Ruddy.

C O W T O W N

Cattle Trails And West Bottom Tales

* *

A symbol of the tie between railroad and cattle men is the bell from the Kansas City Southern Belle steam-engine on a post on the old Kaney farm in Lee's Summit where Sally lives today. William Deramus II, president of the Kansas City Southern Railway, removed the bell from the Southern Belle's engine after its inaugural trip to New Orleans in 1940 and gave it to Cliff Kaney. Now Cliff's grandson calls his horses to their stable in the evenings by ringing that bell.

Photo courtesy of Sally Ruddy

C O W T O W N

Cattle Trails And West Bottom Tales

Cliff Kaney on a Monday morning at the stockyards
Photo courtesy of Sally Ruddy

C O W T O W N

Cattle Trails And West Bottom Tales

Sally was very grateful for the security of her own home, provided by her father's stockyard work, and quick to defend the yards. Whenever a teacher called on Sally's class to tell what their fathers did to earn a living, the more likely response was that he worked in an office downtown. When Sally said her father was a cattleman at the stockyards, most of her classmates held their noses. This offended Sally, who told them that the class should take a field trip to see how clean the stockyard pens were kept and how sweet the straw in those pens smelled.

> "On Saturdays the pens would be empty at the stockyards. They would be clean and covered with sweet-smelling hay and straw. Monday morning when the market opened the pens would be full of cattle and men on horseback moving through them. Young men would be on hand to swing the gates open and close them again as directed. Large hooks fastened gates open or held them closed. The pens could be arranged to make into any size required." Sally Ruddy.

Robert Morris remembers the West Bottoms smell.

> "That verdant, reeking, subhuman, terrifying smell of slaughterhouse and manure, alfalfa and wet sheep's wool, mule piss and man's sweat - all rising up in a sweltering, dusty July cloud that swirled above the rank intermingling of the Kaw and Missouri rivers below. Despite its raucousness, its color and the high spirits of the men, I knew what the shouts of 'Cudahy, "Armour,' 'Wilson,' 'Swift and Company,' at the scale meant. This was one big zone devoted to death. The stockyards were a living funnel into those charnel-house holes." The Stockyard Shaman, supra.

West Bottoms residents and neighbors had no problem with the aroma. It was the smell of money, and they became so accustomed to it that they hardly noticed it.

COWTOWN

Cattle Trails And West Bottom Tales

THE FRATERNITY

Built upon an atmosphere of trust, stockyard business practices may have been informal but they were no less effective. Sometimes two buyers had an interest in the same lot of cattle and the right to choose first was determined by a coin flip. If there were three or more contenders, numbers or straws were drawn by them from a hat to determine priority, often without them leaving their saddles.

Drawing Straws for First Pick
Photo by Hylite Inc., courtesy of James Runyan, Jr.

C O W T O W N

Cattle Trails And West Bottom Tales

The coin flip was also available to resolve other differences. Once, Cliff Kaney was talking on his home phone long distance with a customer with cattle to sell. The customer wanted a higher price than Cliff had offered and Cliff, sitting in the Kaney sun room, said "We'll flip for it. You want heads or tails?" Then he asked "Who flips?" Then he flipped a coin. Next he said "You win. You get your price." Sally Ruddy, who witnessed Cliff s end of the episode, suspected that the seller was going to win the flip in any event, in the interest of good customer relations.

There was a friendship among the stockyards fraternity that manifested itself on occasions. One such occasion was the result of Cliff Kaney's collapse with a bleeding ulcer. Sally and her mother rushed to Saint Luke's Hospital where Kaney was awaiting a blood transfusion. As they sat in the hospital emergency room, men in Stetsons and boots began to collect there. The word was out in the stockyards that Cliff Kaney urgently needed a blood donor and these were prospective donors. When a line formed, Jewish mule dealer Morris Studna pushed to the front, declaring "what that Irishmen needs is some good Jewish blood." And that is what Kaney received.

Robert Morris saw the stockyards camaraderie in a locker room environment:

> "Father was a livestock man. Mother thought it was a bad influence on me to go down to the stockyards. This provided incentive enough for me to go every chance I got. Father himself was transformed body and soul upon entering this malodorous and exotic zone. The men who worked in the stockyards arrived in drab and proper attire and ascended the worn stairs to Orrin Haggard's locker room. Here, these ordinary-looking men metamorphosed, donning their variously shaped Stetsons, their lizard boots, their pearlsnapped shirts, chaps and straps and double belts and Mexican spurs with rowels the size of silver dollars. And all of this amidst clouds of steam and talcum powder, the yelling, the elaborate obscenities, the bookmaking, the cigar smoke and the rattle and snap of snooker balls. There, witnessing cattle whips and wet towels flicked at unguarded rears, the boasting, the cursing and the execution of flamboyant, three-cushion side-pocket shots at the green pool tables, I knew I had entered a different — a secret — zone. There, Father glowed beneath his Stetson. I could see that he was far more at home there than at home...."The Stockyard Shaman

COWTOWN

Cattle Trails And West Bottom Tales

Another member of the fraternity was Carl Strobel. He was the head cattle buyer for Swift & Company and told a newspaper reporter that he "enjoyed every day of it."

> "You're trading thousands of dollars, but in a friendly way. They want to sell as high as they can and I want to buy as low as I can. But it's not like uptown. If you were spending that kind of money there each side would have a couple of lawyers. Here I just nod my head and say 'weigh 'em to Swift' and that's all there is to it. The seller comes around in the afternoon and his money is there."
> Kansas City Star, October 22, 1965.

A packing house buyer such as Carl Strobel purchased livestock for slaughter, and could estimate to within a few pounds how much each animal would weigh when "dressed out" (slaughtered and processed). The 40-year career of Dollie Levi at Swift & Company was largely devoted to assessing the accuracy of Strobel's statements. "Aunt Dollie told me that the buyers on horseback estimated the yield from a pen of cattle they purchased and it was her job to keep track of how those estimates compared with actual outcomes." Morton Sosland.

Scene in Stock Yards, Kansas City, Mo.

Buyer and seller negotiating the price
Ray Postcard Collection

92

C O W T O W N

Cattle Trails And West Bottom Tales

THE DILLINGHAMS

In 1937 Jay B. Dillingham, native Missourian and law school graduate, came to the Kansas City Stock Yards Company as assistant to the vice president. Jay was no stranger...he had been a "gofer" who helped organize the Royal's spring horse show, among other things. He would later serve as Company president for 27 years, and the yards and environs would profit greatly from his aggressive, progressive leadership.

The Jay B. Dillingham Award for Agricultural Leadership & Excellence is presented annually by the Agricultural Business Council of Kansas City. The inspiration for the glass hat award came from Jay Dillingham's trademark Stetson hat.

Photo courtesy of John Dillingham

COWTOWN

Cattle Trails And West Bottom Tales

The importance of the stockyards in the business community had been demonstrated earlier by Cliff Kaney's election as president of the Kansas City, Missouri Chamber of Commerce. Kaney was also lauded in a Kansas City Star editorial (January 21, 1960) for his performance as the Metropolitan Area Planning Council's first president.

Jay Dillingham likewise became chairman of the Kansas City, Missouri Chamber of Commerce and was elected chairman of the Kansas City, Kansas Chamber as well, bridging the gap between the twin cities. The massive, heavily-traveled Dillingham Freeway Bridge (Interstate 670 viaduct) over the West Bottoms which connects both municipalities is his monument. When Missouri officials named their end of the bridge after Dillingham there was some question as to whether Kansans would follow suit but they did and appropriately the entire span between the twin cities was dedicated to him.

According to Bruce Mathews (Kansas City Spirit, supra), "Jay Dillingham frequently remarked that it was surely a 'sign' that he and the Livestock Exchange Building were 'born', as he put it, in the same year, 1910." Dillingham also wrote the definitive history of the yards' earlier years, The History of the Kansas City Livestock Market And The Kansas City Stock Yards Company 1871-1985.

Jay was not the first Dillingham in the stockyards. In Cuthbert Powell's book, supra, there are a biographical sketch and picture of W. J. Dillingham of Clay County, Missouri.

> "W. J. Dillingham has long been one of the conspicuous young men in the yards, commencing in the early days of the trade here, and having served in every capacity from yardman to salesman, and filled the latter responsibility when only twenty-one years of age...Through all his ups and downs 'Joe' Dillingham, as he is known to his intimates, has always been cheerful and ever willing to fight the battle of life honestly and fairly whether for or against him."

According to the May 1, 1886 issue of the Kansas City Illustrated Review, the firm of Dillingham and Hudson officed then in room 3 of the Livestock Exchange Building, and W. J. Dillingham had "for over seven years been regarded as one of the most energetic and thoroughly posted men in the business."

Cattle Trails And West Bottom Tales

Jay was not the last stockyard Dillingham either...his son John is a worthy successor. At the age of nine John began his long stockyard career with the sale of a calf to Edgar Weil, owner and operator of the Central Packing Company. Characteristically, Weil did not dismount from his horse for the transaction. Jay Dillingham was an interested witness, and when Weil's first offer was inadequate Jay suggested to John that he "invite Mr. Weil to get down from his horse for a closer look." Weil dismounted, and peered, and agreement was reached.

A proud Wentworth Cadet, John Dillingham attended the Chamber of Commerce dinner when his father was
inducted as the Missouri chamber's new president.
Photo courtesy of John Dillingham

John, a member of the 4H Club who exhibited in cattle auctions, found saying good-by to his Angus steer calves Fat Stuff and Big Stuff to be wrenching. He had raised, groomed and fed them, and after their sale at auction "their halters were removed and I walked away, knowing their fate." It's All About Eating, supra.

COWTOWN

Cattle Trails And West Bottom Tales

In 1949, in a hallway just outside the Golden Ox, ten-year-old John Dillingham watched WDAF-TV newscaster Randall Jessee interview his father. It was Kansas City's first live television broadcast.

Today, John Dillingham is president and CEO of Dillingham Enterprises with offices on the 9th floor of the Livestock Exchange Building. In his office is a worn "fainting couch", relic of a bygone age when one of these was to be found in every lady's restroom in the building. There is also a spittoon from a men's restroom — the cowboys were made of sterner stuff.

Ladies' lounges with "fainting couches"
Ray postcard collection

The rooms of the Hoof and Horn Club were once located down the hall to the north. An August 8, 1946 article by the Kansas City Star's Howard Turtle briefly described these precincts:

> "At the exclusive Hoof and Horn Club, thickly spread with green carpeting that bore occasional wisps of hay and straw from the members' shoes, executives looked out the west windows across the pens of mooing, shifting cattle..."

Posted at the Club entrance was a list of rules, 37 of them. Rule Two: "no game shall be played on a Sunday, nor shall any game of any kind or description be allowed in the Club Rooms." Tipping was prohibited, as was loud conversation in the Library or Rest Rooms. And there was a credit limit of $25, with all indebtedness to the Club paid on or before the 10th day of each month. Failure to pay by the 15th resulted in "conspicuous" posting of the name of a delinquent. Framed copy of rules provided courtesy of Golden Ox.

COWTOWN

Cattle Trails And West Bottom Tales

A corner office on the south end of the 9th floor was occupied by the president of the Stockyards Company, and nearby was the Exchange Hall, a meeting room. Both are office spaces today.

John Dillingham eats lunch often at "his" table in the Golden Ox, surrounded by many artifacts and art works donated to the Ox by his father. He is also a historian of note, with a historian's interest not only in the stockyards but also in his own illustrious family. Not just on his father's side did his family play a major role in stockyards history, but on his mother's side as well. His maternal grandfather, Allen M. Thompson, was president of the American Royal the year it was incorporated, 1905, and served the Royal and the stockyards in many other important capacities.

Photo courtesy of Golden Ox Restaurant

C O W T O W N

Cattle Trails And West Bottom Tales

A MISSOURI MULE IN THE MOVIES

In September of 1899 an English agent visited Kansas City and purchased 20 Missouri mules for the British army. And during World War I, Kansas City-based Guyton and Harrington sold 350,000 horses and mules to the British army to pull ambulances and supplies. In 1939, fiction borrowed from history when Paramount Studios released a movie starring Champ Clark, the 1937 American Royal grand champion mule named for a former Speaker of the United States House of Representatives from Missouri. The movie was adapted for the screen by a former motion picture editor of the Kansas City Star, John C. Moffitt, and Duke Attebury.

In the film, the Missouri mule market was in a severe slump and some breeders in a small Missouri town, heavily invested in mules, were in desperate financial straits. Possible salvation appeared when British Army officers came to Kansas City seeking mules for their army. A British captain even attended the American Royal but no sale resulted.

The mule, with the screen name of Samson, accompanied by his owner the town banker and 2000 other mules, traveled to London where the British government was trying to decide whether to buy mules or tractors for its colonial troops. The movie had a happy ending: a call from India for army mules resulted in the sale of all the Missouri mules

A full-page spread in the Star complete with pictures provided a brief synopsis of the movie and the role in it of unsuspecting Kansas Citians:

> "'I'm From Missouri', a forthcoming motion picture starring Bob Burns and a Missouri mule, will place upon the screen the countenances of hundreds of persons who attended the American Royal last fall in Kansas City. Probably none of those persons knew he was serving as a screen extra."

98

C O W T O W N

Cattle Trails And West Bottom Tales

EVERYTHING WAS UP TO DATE IN KANSAS CITY

Dr. Ralph Hall, a retired endocrinologist and distinguished medical educator with a home in Evergreen, Colorado, grew up on the great plains of western Kansas, cattle country. Friends of Ralph's youth were Loy (Slick) Oldham and the three sons of rancher Herbert J. Barr. They undertook many expeditions together, often in this 1926 Ford truck – standing are Oldham and Ken Barr, and seated are Bill Barr, Ralph Hall, and at the wheel Jack Barr.

Photo courtesy of Ralph Hall, M.D.

In his essay "To the Kansas City Stock Yards", Ralph Hall described another expedition by the fivesome, an experience shared by scores of other young farmers and ranchers.

The trip's preliminaries were not novel experiences for Ralph and his companions, but anticipation was great.

> "It was a warm early August morning. It was light, but the sun had not shown above the horizon. We headed back, after a breakfast of bacon, eggs and milk, to the large red barn where we teen-age cowboys had spent the night sleeping on a great mound of hay stacked on the upper floor. (World War II was in full swing, so labor of all kinds was in short supply.) The Herbert J. Barr Ranch was 7 miles north and one mile west of the small town of Leoti, Kansas, seat of Wichita County. Kansas City lay 400 miles to the east.

> "Approximately 250 head of cattle had been rounded up and pastured in a fenced-in, grassy area just south of the Barr ranch house during the previous two days. Our job was to drive them to a railroad loading corral, located on a siding of the Missouri Pacific Railroad about a mile west of Leoti.

COWTOWN

Cattle Trails And West Bottom Tales

"There were few fences in Western Kansas in those days. We were able to drive the bawling cattle along a dusty county road. The wheat had been harvested and a new crop of winter wheat would not be planted until late August or September. That allowed the cattle to stray onto the fields along the side of the road without doing any damage. It enabled us to move the cattle with ease toward the railroad siding."

At railroad loading corrals, ranch hands customarily poked cattle with long prods to drive them up chutes into cattle cars — hence the cowboy nickname "cowpoke."

"We arrived at the siding in the hot mid-afternoon and as soon as we arrived began loading the cattle into the cattle cars. They were prodded through a chute that led up to the car's entrance, and once one or two of them went into a car the others followed.

"There was no engine to move the cattle cars; a long, crow-bar-like pole was placed between the wheel and the rail, and the car edged forward while someone managed the brakes. It was a slow, dusty, noisy process. We finished the loading in time to go into town for dinner and return to the cars so we would be there when the train that was to attach the cattle cars arrived. We were tired but excited since we would be riding in the caboose to the Kansas City Stock Yards with the cattle.

"The railroad allotted one passenger per car of cattle to travel with the train. Our job was to monitor the cattle to make certain they were not harming each other and had a supply of water. We cowboys had a secondary agenda which had not been discussed...we wanted to go to the Folly Theatre in Kansas City."

Travel was educational for the young cowpokes.

"When the train had attached the loaded cars, we climbed aboard the caboose. The conductor in charge of the train had quarters in the small loft that rose above the main roof of the caboose. He immediately made it clear that that was his private domain and we were to confine ourselves to the plastic covered benches along the inside walls of the caboose. We were so tired we could have slept anywhere at the beginning of the trip.

"Leoti was only 36 miles from the Colorado State Line. The train began moving once the west-bound Colorado Eagle streamliner passed. It seemed like a long night because we kept stopping on side tracks to let other, higher priority trains pass. We didn't arrive at the transfer station in Hoisington, Kansas until just before noon the following day. We had time to eat since this was the place where the crew changed.

"We checked all the cattle cars, filled their troughs with water, and returned to meet the new conductor. He was a very talkative man in his 40s. Shortly after we were under way, he came down to our area of the caboose and after some small talk proceeded to

COWTOWN

Cattle Trails And West Bottom Tales

enlighten us about his active sex life and to provide us with information about Kansas City that our folks would not have approved of.

"We continued to stop frequently that night in order to let other trains pass. The benches had become very uncomfortable beds by this time. It took us 24 hours to reach Kansas City. The train moved more slowly as we approached the Bottoms. We had reservations at the West End Hotel and the conductor advised us to jump off the moving train just before we arrived at the stock yards. We would be close to our hotel. This we did without difficulty."

The sights, sounds and smells of the stockyards were all too familiar. There were other educational opportunities, however, as noted by Richard Rogers and Oscar Hammerstein in "Oklahoma": "I went to Kansas City on a Friday. By Saturday I learned a thing or two." (Everything's Up to Date in Kansas City).

"We had been told about the Cowboy Inn Bar near the hotel, and went there for lunch. Two of our group ordered liquor; their orders were taken without any question. The rest of us had cokes and sandwiches."

More from "Oklahoma": "They got a big theatre they call a burlesque, for fifty cents you could see a dandy show."

"After lunch we walked up the hill to the main part of the city where we found what we were looking for - the Folly Theatre.

"We were in time for the afternoon performance, but the sign above the box office said that no one under 18 years of age would be admitted. After a short conference we gave money for our tickets to Slick Oldham, who was tall, dark, and had enough facial hair to appear to be 18. We borrowed a cigarette from a bystander. Slick took the cigarette to the box office where he dropped it and ground it out with his foot, looking every bit of 18. He casually purchased five tickets."

"Although the Folly show was supposed to be very risqué, it paled beside anything that can currently be seen on television. The vaudeville acts were clever and fun, and we had a great time.

"We stayed at the West End Hotel that night."

And then the return to Leoti, Kansas.

"The next day we boarded the Colorado Eagle for the journey home. The tickets were provided by the Missouri Pacific Railroad for passengers that had accompanied cattle being shipped to the stock yards on one of their trains.

101

C O W T O W N

Cattle Trails And West Bottom Tales

"It was a successful and memorable trip." Ralph Hall, M.D.

****

William Kircher Esq., an attorney with Kansas City's Husch Blackwell law firm who specializes in intellectual property law, grew up on a Missouri farm. The Kirchers' crops included pigs. Bill's father prized physical fitness, and challenged his son to lift 100 pounds by his 10th birthday. He then introduced him to a readily available training regimen – pig lifting. The program began one day with the lifting of a very young pig and entailed its daily hoisting as it gradually gained size and weight. By the time the pig, and the program, reached maturity, and before Bill was 10 years old, he was lifting a squirming 100 pounds.

Kircher pigs were trucked to the Kansas City stockyards, where they were sold. Bill recalls a subsequent visit to the Folly theatre and a performance there by famed fan dancer Sally Rand – who performed at the Chicago World's Fair in 1934. "Now that was a big deal for a farm/ranch hand from Bates County, Missouri." Bill Kircher.

****

The Folly Theatre, now well over 100 years old, has gone from performances of "the ol' bump and grind" to chamber music and listing on the National Register of Historic Places, thanks in large measure to the preservation efforts of Joan Dillon.

Folly Theatre
Steve Noll Photo

Folly Theatre Headliner
Missouri Valley Collection

COWTOWN

Cattle Trails And West Bottom Tales

WORLD WAR II

During World War II, Kansas City's agribusiness was more important than ever as part of the war effort. Farmers couldn't get gas or tires, so everything was shipped by rail. Horse-drawn conveyances circulated among the railroad terminals. The American Royal building was occupied by the Commonwealth Aircraft Company for the production of gliders. The Darby Products of Steel Company on the banks of the Kaw manufactured thousands of landing craft. Packing house production reached new highs, furnishing rations for the best-fed armed forces in history. In an S. J. Ray cartoon in the Star (October, 1943), a Kansas City businessman and a cowboy's ghost celebrated the biggest cattle run ever. The cartoon was entitled: "Still the Greatest Cow Town in America."

STILL THE GREATEST COW-TOWN IN AMERICA.

COWTOWN

Cattle Trails And West Bottom Tales

The Columbian Steel Tank Company was a major contributor to the war effort as manufacturer of steel tanks for the storage and truck transport of oil and gasoline. It became virtually a government enterprise, using large quantities of precious steel and employing some 850 people in a facility covering three square blocks.

Forty-four khaki-clad stockyard rangers on horseback provided wartime armed guards for the yards. Their captain, Fred Olander, had been a field artillery captain in World War I. He served twice as president of the National Livestock Exchange and four times as president of the Kansas City Livestock Exchange. A tall, imposing man who had once aspired to the ministry, he officiated at funerals of more than 40 stockmen. His father, a Swedish immigrant named Jonathan Wilhelm Olander, had been a livestock commission merchant in the stockyards, followed about the pens at the yard by young Frederick. Jonathon's grandson, Fred Olander Jr., was a POW during the war after his bomber was shot down over Germany. When Fred Sr. died in 1971, the Kansas City Times wrote: "In the years when the cattle business was booming in Kansas City no name was more immediately connected with the stockyards than that of the Olanders."

Ferdinand (Ferd) Lincoln Owen moved to Kansas City from Joplin, Missouri and opened a trading barn with a sign offering "Ferd Owen Mules.".a sign that could be seen there long after his retirement. He bought low and sold high, and in the process became the biggest mule and horse trader in the United States. In May, 1943, Ferd Owen received a letter from a cavalry officer with the Quartermaster Corps to the effect that the Army wanted all the pack mules Ferd could produce. "Upon our ability, with your help, to procure, and supply to the fighting units the animals needed, may depend the success or failure of a campaign against our enemies."

The letter concluded: "You are authorized to use this letter as evidence to your local rationing board of the essential nature and importance of your part in the procurement program, should it be necessary, in order to obtain gasoline for your buyers. However, it is requested that the facts be given as little publicity as possible." Copy of letter provided courtesy of Ferdinand Good, grandson of Ferd Owen.

Commercial realtor Jerry Fogel later profited from his wartime entertainment in the stockyards.

> "My grandfather, a friend of Jay Dillingham's, took me on a tour of the stockyards in 1945 when I had short pants and short legs. Dad was in the Navy at the time and Grandpa occasionally entertained me and it was his idea. You can only imagine my awe at all those cows and cowboys.

> "In 1966, I dealt with a director of real estate for General Motors Corp who was a breeder of cattle on the side. I bravely felt I could walk him through the stockyards as I had been years before. He was so impressed that he made all his future deals in Kansas City through me as a real estate broker." Jerry Fogel.

In August 1945, the war came to an end. Swift & Henry announced that the price on some classes of cattle had fallen rather badly because "packers all over the country got behind in their kill two weeks ago when the packing house help took a day or two off to celebrate the end of the war." The announcement also noted that James L. Runyan had been employed as cattle salesman and vice president. Runyan would be joined at the firm by his son, James Jr., who today owns and operates Swift & Henry Order Buying Company.

James M. Kemper Jr. had placed 3rd in the American Royal's boys and girls jumping class in 1929. An accomplished horseman, he was inducted as a horse cavalry volunteer in July 1942. Kemper recalls "That branch of the service was full of horse athletes like jockeys, horse trainers, polo players, cowboys and Western ranch types." Now, he was back from the war after distinguished service with the 1st Cavalry Division's 8th Cavalry. Despite the name, it was a mechanized outfit. "For anyone who loved horses, being in the horse cavalry was a great experience, but it was no way to fight a modern war." (James M. Kemper Jr.) Upon his return, Jim Kemper served briefly as president of the Stock Yards National Bank, an affiliate of the Commerce Trust Company. His grandfather, William Thornton Kemper, was an original shareholder and director of the Stock Yards National. Another Kemper bank in 1897 absorbed the former Armour Brothers Banking Company founded by the meatpacking family. Jim later became Chairman and CEO of Commerce Bancshares.

James M. Kemper, Jr.
Photo from "The Pursuit of a Ruptured Duck"

Demand With Victories

WAR SUCCESSES are bringing a revival in flour buying for foreign relief. As the liberated areas in Europe expand and as more shipping space becomes available with military gains for the Allies, government buying for relief is increasing. In recent months lack of shipping space retarded the movement for relief abroad.

Tightness in supplies experienced last winter, when government buying was very heavy, may recur. Domestic consumers should take steps to guard against such a situation in flour.

COWTOWN

Cattle Trails And West Bottom Tales

BILL HORNER

In 1946, thirteen-year-old Bill Horner found employment in the stockyards with his uncle, Fred Olander. He was paid 45 cents per hour and put to work cleaning pens, and opening and closing alley and pen gates. The second year a sympathetic bookkeeper provided an unauthorized 10- cent-per-hour raise.

Bill's third day on the job, he overheard an argument in a cattle chute overhead, followed by the thump of a body falling to the pen floor nearby. The victim did not survive the fall. Bill learned that the dead man had been in a crap game and was thrown over the chute's rail by another crap shooter. Both were among the derelicts that hung around the yards and found temporary employment "pushing" cattle and working the gates. These men were paid a dollar or two for their help, money they used to buy "sweet Lucy" — a cheap wine available at a nearby liquor store. There was no subsequent investigation of the death — their lives were also cheap.

Organized labor issues rarely reached the stockyards in those years. The men in the pens and alleys were not then union men, although they "bitched about hours and pay" to Horner. Union organizers who ventured into the yards often received a hostile reception. On one occasion a sack of wet flour dropped from an upper floor of the Livestock Exchange building broke the neck of a union organizer. The identity of the perpetrators was well known among the men in the yards but never disclosed to investigators.

Fred Olander warned his young nephew against turning his back on livestock enclosed with him in a pen or alley. The wisdom of the advice was brought home by a near miss from a charging, horned mother cow early in Bill's stockyard days, and never forgotten.

Bill accompanied Fred on his business trips and observed many of the same transactions as Sally Ruddy. Meticulous preparations always included placing a satchel full of blank contracts in the back seat of the car. However, Bill never saw any of the contracts removed from the satchel, much less actually put to use. The transactions remained verbal, based on the customary handshake.

Cattlemen kept a change of clothes in open lockers at Orrin Haggard's Locker Room, located in a building across Genesee Street from the Livestock Exchange building. Shoes and boots were placed under lockers, for cleaning. Bill recalls that, over time, small mountains of rock-hard manure collected on the floor, impervious to removal.

Bill Horner

COWTOWN

Cattle Trails And West Bottom Tales

OLE FERD OWEN

On July 1947, Kansas City's Ferd Owen came under fire from fellow mule dealers. South of the border, Mexican work oxen were being slaughtered to eradicate hoof and mouth disease decimating Mexican herds. The United States Congress authorized a cooperative project wherein the Mexican oxen were to be replaced by first-class American mules that were not susceptible to the disease. The Department of Agriculture notified all the big mule dealers that it wanted to buy mules for resale in Mexico but there followed prolonged price negotiations between the Department and Mexican officials. While negotiations dragged on, an impatient Owen flew to Mexico and came back with a contract to sell to the Mexican Government 20,000 mules at $115 a head, a handsome price. That maneuver cornered the Mexican market, just about eliminating everyone else.

Ferd's competitors were outraged. Some of them talked to their Congressmen and a bill was drafted to delay Owen's transaction until they could get in on the bonanza. But the anti-Ferd mule legislation never reached Congress.

Ferd's grandson and namesake, Ferdinand Good, is the source of many other Ferd Owen stories. One has to do with another 1947 international incident. Owen had sold a large number of Missouri mules to the Spanish government of prime-minister Francisco Franco. Franco remitted payment and three ships were tied up at a loading dock, ready to transport them, but there was a delay caused by U.S. officials concerned with the elevated temperatures of the mules waiting on loading ...a condition that the exasperated Ferd Owen attributed to the hot sun and lack of water endured as they waited. As the wait grew longer, Ferd finally placed a long distance call to a fan of Missouri mules, President Harry S Truman. (On Missouri Day at the Royal in 1963, there was a special mule exhibition and Harry Truman rode around the ring on a mule-drawn wagon.) The President promptly connected Ferd with the Secretary of Agriculture. Clearance came immediately. Franco got his mules.

Kansas City Horse & Mule Commission Co.
1735 Wyoming   Owned and Operated by Ferd Owen

COWTOWN

Cattle Trails And West Bottom Tales

President Truman greeting a mule and its exhibitor, Joey O'Brien age 12, from Hiatville, KS
Photo Courtesy of Harry S Truman Library

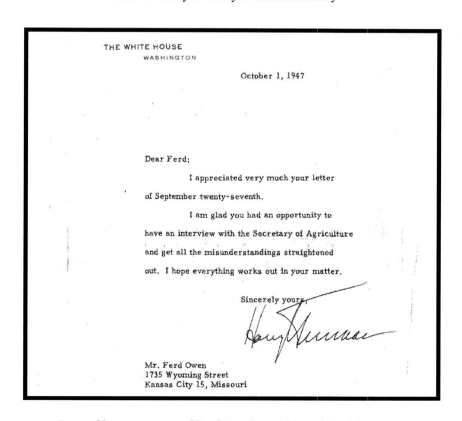

THE WHITE HOUSE
WASHINGTON

October 1, 1947

Dear Ferd:

I appreciated very much your letter of September twenty-seventh.

I am glad you had an opportunity to have an interview with the Secretary of Agriculture and get all the misunderstandings straightened out. I hope everything works out in your matter.

Sincerely yours,

Harry Truman

Mr. Ferd Owen
1735 Wyoming Street
Kansas City 15, Missouri

Copy of letter courtesy of Ferd Good, grandson of Ferd Owen

COWTOWN

Cattle Trails And West Bottom Tales

ORGANIZE!

According to Edwin Shutt's Armour Family History, supra, "from the 1880s until 1900 the meatpacking industry was probably the most strife-ridden industry in the country." The publication of Upton Sinclair's classic muckraker "The Jungle" followed a failed 1904 meatpackers' strike. Intended to expose the working conditions of Chicago's meatpacking workers, the book also led to passage of the federal Food and Drug Act and the Meat Inspection Act.

A message near the end of The Jungle exhorted: "Organize! Organize! Organize!" And packing house laborers everywhere did, joining unions.

The West Bottoms had its share of packing house labor unrest and union disputes, beginning well before the turn of the 20th century.

> "In 1893, packinghouse strikes landed combative Irish, native and Negro workers on the street. Management of the five local packinghouse operations brought in replacement workers, including many newly-arrived Slavs." From the Bottom Up, Pat O'Neill, supra.

One 17-year-old Slavic replacement, Anton Horvat, recruited in 1908 to replace strikers, went to work at Armours. "He worked there till the day he died, literally right on the steps of the plant." Bernadette Soptick.

G. Edmonds Mackey became manager of the Armour plant in 1946, and shortly afterward experienced a bitter strike. He and company attorney W. Coleman Branton spent uncomfortable nights sleeping at the plant because of violence. They smuggled workers past the picket lines in the trunks of cars that were the targets of pickets' bricks. Mackey sent his family to St. Louis relatives, pending settlement of the strike.

In 1959, Maurer-Neuer Inc., a meat packer with a plant in the West Bottoms, sued to recover damages from the United Packinghouse Workers of America, a labor organization affiliated with the AFL-CIO. Both were parties to a collective bargaining agreement that had a no-strike provision but despite this the union set up picket lines and encouraged a strike by company employees.

Labor problems such as these contributed to the later relocation of West Bottom meat packers.

COWTOWN

Cattle Trails And West Bottom Tales

SOME AMERICAN ROYAL SUPPORTERS

The loyal support of many individuals and organizations has been crucial to the survival, not to mention the success, of the American Royal.

The Saddle & Sirloin Club was founded in 1940 to boost the livestock industry in general and the American Royal in particular. The Club was formally organized at the Swift & Company plant during a sirloin dinner hosted by the plant manager. Saddle & Sirloin Club History, 1940- 1990, Bill and Sue Symon.

Club "trail rides" to Cheyenne's Frontier Days, San Antonio's Fiesta San Jacinto, and New Orleans' Fiesta were among many public relations triumphs. These expeditions were not Spartan affairs: for Operation Santa Fe (New Mexico) in 1947, the Santa Fe Railroad provided 2 dining cars, 10 sleeping cars for 180 people, and freight cars for horses, tack and wagons.

Operation Santa Fe, 1947
Photo courtesy of the Saddle & Sirloin Club

Horses were trucked to Memphis in 1954 where the Saddle & Sirloin Color Guard led the Cotton Carnival Parade and TV's Wild Bill Hickok (Guy Madison) joined the Club's Mounted Patrol.

111

COWTOWN

Cattle Trails And West Bottom Tales

The legendary John E. Miller rode in the American Royal Parade with the Saddle & Sirloin Patrol beginning in 1941 and continued to do so for the next half century.

Financial support for the Royal and participation in its events by the Club over the years have been significant.

****

Harry Darby, United States Senator from Kansas and one-time Kaw River landing craft manufacturer, was American Royal president from 1941 to 1952, and the Royal was one of his top priorities. He was able to attract many luminaries to Royal events. Two Darby sons-in-law, Ray Evans and Roy A. Edwards Jr., prominent in their own right, served as American Royal presidents.

****

Dwight Sutherland was a Royal president and, in 1999, an honorary chairman of the American Royal Centennial. The Sutherland Lumber Co. opened its stockyards facility in 1936 across the street from the Royal building, and Dwight and his brother John became associated with the Royal at an early age. Sally Ruddy envied them:

> "When I was in Bryant elementary school with classmates John and Dwight Sutherland, I attended the Royal every night with my parents. Cars parked in a lot behind the Royal building and had to leave by driving through the alley that was part of the Sutherland Lumber Company's lumber yard in the West Bottoms. I remember waving at my classmates Dwight and John from the back seat of my parents' car. They looked so important as they stood in the alley with their flash lights waving the cars along their way." Sally Ruddy.

****

In 1949, ten men and women (one of them Harry Darby) founded the Belles of the American Royal (BOTAR) as a way to interest young people in promoting the Royal. As Senator Darby reasoned: "We knew if we had the girls we would get the boys." The first BOTARs were presented at a Coronation Ball, and their appearance in the American Royal Parade was covered by Life Magazine. Their western wear was borrowed from members of the Saddle & Sirloin Club.

There was a BOTAR age limitation, years 21 to 27. Their escorts had to be 22 to 31 years of age. Proposers of escorts could only be BOTARS, although in several romantic instances the tables were turned with escorts later proposing to BOTARS. Since then, BOTARS have supported the American Royal by fostering community interest, providing volunteer services, and raising funds.

The BOTAR Fiftieth Anniversary Book, 1949 - 1999, was written by Amy Haun and Mary Soden. There Virginia Jennings Nadeau remembers that in the 50's BOTARs were reminded to wear gloves in public. And Laura Hockaday recalls that in 1960 when some of the ostrich feathers from her big fan caught in the mouth of escort Carl Bolte, she asked him if he was "feeling a little down in the mouth." By 1999, the American Royal's Centennial year, the BOTARS had donated over $1,250,000 to the Royal.

1963 BOTAR Ball, in Municipal Auditorium
Kansas City Star photo, courtesy of Linda Cook.

****

Eddie Williams (Williams Meat Company) was often the high bidder for grand champion steers and lambs at auctions. Other purchasers included Williams' brother-in-law Jud Putsch (Putsch's 210 Restaurant), the Golden Ox, and J.C. Penny. The goal of the auction was to raise money for the education of the youth who raised the champion, and the auctioneer conspired with bidders in the audience to inflate the purchase price.

Sally would have her turn in the spotlight. A November 1940 Kansas City Star American Royal ad was a photographic montage including a David Douglas Duncan picture of Southwest High School drum majorette Sally Ruddy and photos of Western movie star Leo Carrillo who would lead that year's American Royal Parade, and champion Hereford bull Royal Rupert.

COWTOWN

Cattle Trails And West Bottom Tales

1940 American Royal Advertisement
Kansas City Star

American Royal president Dwight Sutherland receiving a check from BOTAR president Janelle Coulson, 1984. American Royal general manager Laurence Pressley stands between Mr. Sutherland and Mrs. Coulson. Robert D. Hovey is at right.

Photo courtesy American Royal Association

COWTOWN

Cattle Trails And West Bottom Tales

THE LIVESTOCK EXCHANGE BUILDING AND "THE OX"

The May 9, 1949 edition of the Daily Drovers Telegram announced the imminent opening of a new "dining and refreshment establishment" in the Livestock Exchange Building, "The Golden Ox." Adjoining it was the "Cow-Town Coffee Shop." The operator, William F Nast, explained the names:

> "The names Cow-Town and Golden Ox are in honor of the people who have made Kansas City the leading livestock center this side of the Mississippi river, and of the rancher and feeder who raise and produce the finest meat anywhere in the world."

Nast emphasized that all would be welcomed in any part of the restaurant or coffee shop..."Whether in chaps or tux, you will be welcomed." And a meal at the Ox, "where the steak was born", became a staple in cattlemen's diets.

Today, Western art adorns the Golden Ox walls including a panoramic cattle drive painting, and oxen yokes, longhorn steer horns, and other memorabilia.

The Golden Ox is a West Bottoms institution, an integral part of the Livestock Exchange Building and located off the main lobby of the building. A big door in the rear of the lobby leads to a parking lot — space that formerly housed the maze of cattle, hog and sheep pens, alleys, barns and Fairbanks scale structures that constituted the stockyards.

Near the exit to the parking lot is a small room furnished with tables and chairs and old stockyard pictures. There are two dominant features: a large blackboard on one wall and, facing it on another wall, a large map of the stockyards as they existed in December of 1897.

The blackboard was part of a marketing news service provided by the United States Department of Agriculture — a scoreboard where occupants of the building and visitors would gather to check livestock prices around the country. The service gave everyone equal access to the same information.

The 1897 map portrays the stockyards of that time — the Livestock Exchange Building bisected by the Missouri-Kansas state line, mule barns, scale locations, hay barns, tool house, lumber yards, numerous railroad tracks, and all of the other structures and facilities comprising a thriving market place.

There was once a cigar stand just inside the building's rear door, offering for sale the chewing tobacco favored over cigars and cigarettes by many men in the livestock business. Cattlemen were out in the dust all day and a chew kept down that dust. Red Man and Beech Nut were big sellers, and clean and polished spittoons decorated every office floor. There was also an umbrella stand filled with canes and whips...replacements if a cattleman heading out the back door had forgotten or broken his own. Just outside that rear door still stands a boot scraper with water faucets attached, and on the exterior wall above hang boot brushes. Booted cattlemen entering the building were expected to make use of these facilities before entering the restaurant or offices inside. Those cattlemen with mud on their boots had wives who'd spend hundreds of dollars in uptown department stores or on Kansas City's Country Club Plaza.

Most of the cattlemen wore boots from Shipley's, where lasts of their boot size were kept on file so they could conveniently order a perfect fit. Even in dress clothes, some wore black boots, disguised by a regular heel and round toe. They claimed that otherwise their ankles were cold.

* * * * * * * * * * * *

The Livestock Exchange Building is on "Genessee" Street, according to today's street signs. It is the principal thoroughfare in the one-time stockyards area.

The 1897 map spells "Genesee" with one "s" whereas the 1907 map by Dodd, Mead & Co. at p. 3 above spells it with a double "s."

The schizophrenia was pervasive: for example a 1914 Jackson County Real Estate Atlas has both spellings on the same page and 1925 Kansas City, Missouri Atlas uses one spelling in the Index and the other elsewhere in the book.

It appears to be an Iroquois Indian word. The Iroquois were a confederacy of several peoples in central New York, but one branch – the Cherokee – originated in Tennessee and North Carolina, and later spread to Oklahoma and Texas. In their language, Genessee (double "s") meant "the beautiful valley." However, another Iroquois branch, the Senecas, spelled it Genesee (single "s") but had a similar meaning, "pleasant valley."

Perhaps those Indians who traded with trappers, hunters and farmers in the West Bottoms brought with them the word – in those years it was indeed a beautiful, pleasant valley. Small wonder that there has been confusion over spelling during the generations that followed.

COWTOWN

Cattle Trails And West Bottom Tales

THE FLOOD OF 1951

In 1951 there was another flood; this one, the most devastating of all, marked the beginning of the end for the Kansas City stockyards and meatpacking giants. The demise would be slow but inevitable.

The Research and Budget Department of the City of Kansas City, Missouri prepared and published a 186-page story of the flood as seen by reporters and photographers and as presented to the people of Kansas City by the Kansas City Star and Kansas City Times. (Copy provided courtesy of Janet Redhefer Russell). An article written for an eastern newspaper by Star news editor John Colt told "The Whole Story of the Flood."

The Flooded West Bottoms
Missouri Valley Room Photo

The West Bottoms, with their great packing plants and acres of stockyards, housed the American Royal building and another 150 plants and industries as well. The area was protected by dikes over 35 feet high and these were topped by an 8-foot high flood wall of reinforced concrete. There were assurances from the Army engineers that the West Bottoms were safe. Then, about 9:30 the morning of Friday the 13th day of July, the Chief of Army Engineers gave the word that the dikes were giving way. Soon thereafter the Kaw River rolled over the top of the flood wall, a torrent several feet high and traveling at 15 miles an hour.

There was little time to save anything but yourself. Cowboys rode their horses to safety and employees were rescued from the second floor of the Livestock Exchange Building by a hastily assembled fleet of boats.

117

COWTOWN

Cattle Trails And West Bottom Tales

The overhead wooden ramps to the indispensable scales in the stockyards floated off their footings and when they settled down they were left crooked and weak. The Stockyards Company jacked them up but they were never the same as before the flood. The pens and gates all over the yards did not work like they used to, and horseback riders had trouble getting through the gates. Gene Furnish (Maxwell & Furnish).

Some packing houses were back in business before the stockyards resumed operation, and once again packers went into the countryside to buy livestock direct from ranchers and farmers. However, the West Bottoms packing house operations were greatly diminished. Cudahy closed its plant never to return. Wilson Packing Co. left its plant and reopened in a smaller building. Edwin Shutt described the exodus and its cause in his Saga of the Armour Family, supra.

> "During the 1950s and 60s Kansas City began a slow but steady decline as a great meatpacking center. By 1976 all of the 'Big Four' had left Kansas City. Armour began phasing out operations in 1965 and closed its Kansas City plant in 1967. Rising labor and transportation costs were mostly to blame. It was the trend then, as well as now, to build smaller, more efficient plants in towns near the grain- and livestock-producing areas. The era of the great meatpacking families with their huge plants employing thousands of people had come to an end."

****

The West Bottoms area was the economic center and main rail center of the city at a time when the railroads and stockyards were the essence of Kansas City. The flat flood plain was ideal for the passage of trains, and with the arrival of the stockyards and the Livestock Exchange, the area became an essential link, connecting rail traffic from all directions. However the plain had the promise of disaster. Flood damage was a major incentive for the move of the Union Depot to higher ground, a move that coupled with trucks replacing trains led to a large decline in West Bottoms rail traffic.

Photo courtesy of Blueprint For Disaster! Disaster Corps Inc., 1951

118

Cattle Trails And West Bottom Tales

There had been efforts at flood control over the years. In 1933, the Chambers of Commerce of both Kansas Cities created a joint committee on flood control, money was raised by public subscription, and a committee of five was appointed to oversee a continuing effort. One of the members represented the industries and businesses of the "Central Industrial District", a name adopted for the West Bottoms in 1923 by the business organizations of the area. This committee met 132 times in ensuing years in concert with various government agencies.

The Army engineers favored the construction of a giant reservoir upstream to be called the Tuttle Creek Dam. But Kansas farmers did not want to lose their fertile river valley land and every time Tuttle Creek or other proposed dams came before Congress they killed the appropriation. A lesson was finally learned in 1951, however: dikes alone cannot hold a flood and lakes and reservoirs should be constructed upstream to contain unusual rainfall.

****

Bill Horner, now 18 year old, experienced the 1951 flood first-hand. There had been flood warnings, and early the morning of Friday, June 13, Fred Olander's employees gathered in his office to listen to the Army Corps of Engineers' around-the-clock broadcasts reporting river levels and other conditions in the area. There was no prediction of imminent flooding, but Bill "checked out" a horse from a stockyards horse barn and rode over to the 23rd Street Trafficway near the American Royal to see for himself. Here he observed the Kaw River rising rapidly, occasionally splashing over flood walls on the river's east bank. Bill returned to the Olander office to voice concern. His uncle was not convinced, citing Corps of Engineer reassurances. However, Bill continued to monitor the rising water by horseback and finally loaded Fred's two horses on an automobile-drawn trailer, retrieved clothes from Haggard's locker room, and persuaded Fred to exit the yards. As the two fugitives drove up the incline east of the American Royal building, the Kaw River was close behind. Fred Olander, now a believer, told his nephew that he was "smarter than the Corps of Engineers."

William Clark, 21-year-old night shift mechanic at Faultless Starch, had a similar experience. At midnight on July 12, after looking at the river levee protecting the Central Avenue Bridge, a concerned Clark contacted a company official but was told that the levee would hold. "I didn't think it would, so I started moving all the equipment out of the machine shop up to the 2" floor." Clark then went home.

The next morning, Bill Clark returned to see flood water beginning to inundate the Bottoms.

"I drove home and hooked onto my boat, and got back as quickly as I could. Water was now covering the entire area, pushing cars, trucks, rail cars, and a lot of cattle and hogs along with it. I launched my boat and made my way through heavy current and debris to the fire escape on the 1901 building.

"I started taking our people out of the building. It took several trips. Good thing I was young and dumb, or I would have been scared to death! Also, I took several people off the tops of rail cars. Many were so scared I had a real problem trying to get them to wait until I could take out a load and return for them. I had to threaten to hit a couple of them with the boat paddle.

"Channel 4 came down and took film of Tommy Quinn raising the flag on top of the Faultless building." William Clark.

Other West Bottoms commercial operations adjacent to the stockyards suffered damage from the floodwaters, as well. The Gustin Bacon Manufacturing Co., located on 11th Street, suffered $150,000 in damages; a company vice president, finally able to return to his office, found a dead hog on his desk. Harry Darby lost his plant on the west bank of the Kaw.

Flood waters temporarily stilled the "clanging of metal" from the Columbian Steel Tank Company remembered by Robert Morris. Columbian had experienced, and recovered from, the disastrous 1903 flood. Now its tanks, afloat with stowaways on board, drifted to the roof level of the Columbian factory on 12th street in an even greater catastrophe. The resilient plant was soon back in operation however, and remained in the West Bottoms until it was finally put out of business by the construction of the Dillingham Freeway Bridge in 1990. It then relocated in Kansas City, Kansas.

The clanging of metal was stilled
Photo courtesy of Columbian Steel Tank Company (Don Wagner)

Damage reached well beyond the West Bottoms, as Carl Bolte Jr. recalled.

"Dad was vice president of Battenfeld Grease near 31st and Roanoke Road. The night after the flood, we drove to see the Battenfeld property, having to park two blocks south. Walking down the hill north, we arrived at the top of his office. Peering into the murky water, Big Carl told me that there were three oil cars below it, the water engulfing his second-floor office.

C O W T O W N

Cattle Trails And West Bottom Tales

"Returning to his car, we encountered a dead-tired fireman in his wet and smoky uniform. He was trudging toward home. We offered him a ride; he gratefully accepted. Between that point and his home, near 42" and Holly Streets, having been on duty for perhaps 36 hours, the dedicated fireman fell asleep three times."

Carl learned later that another flood loss being mourned was five carloads of Pabst Blue Ribbon beer.

Fred N. Redhefer owned the Great Western Paint Company. Previously located at 6th and Delaware in the West Bottoms, the company was now at 1207 West 11th Street. Business was proceeding at a normal pace there the morning of June 13 when the surprise warning of imminent flooding was received. After the office and factory were evacuated, Redhefer and son-in-law William Russell, a company officer, returned by boat to salvage important office equipment and records from the rising waters. They then retreated to the River Club (founded three years earlier by Redhefer and six other men) and from this vantage point, martinis in hand, they watched the flood waters engulf their building to the second floor window level. Janet Redhefer Russell.

Bill Russell and co-workers clean up the flood debris
Photo courtesy of Janet Redhefer Russell

Another Lewis & Clark Point observer was architect Evans Folger, who knew that a catastrophe was in the making as he watched the water easily top the 14-feet-high doors of a warehouse he had designed.

COWTOWN

Cattle Trails And West Bottom Tales

"Disaster Corps, Inc." was quickly organized by John Massman and others in the construction industry to deal with the devastation. Disaster Corpsmen scoured the West Bottoms for dead animals – the Dead Hog Detail was the busiest. When a policeman ordered them to remove a live hog they refused on jurisdictional grounds:

> "This is a dead hog detail. The livestock boys handle the live ones."

The policeman drew his gun, shot the hog, and said "She's yours." Blueprint for Disaster!

The Swift & Henry office was then on the 2nd floor of the Livestock Exchange Building across the hall from the Stockyards National Bank, with a big, wide staircase in between. The flood waters reached desktops, leaving several inches of awful looking, evil smelling muck. Jim Runyan and another very junior employee were assigned to scoop up the muck and throw it out the office windows onto flood-ravaged Genesee Street. Instead they used a firewater pressure hose in the hallway to wash down the office, resulting in a cataract on the stairway. Their ingenuity was not appreciated by fire and security people, but the result was the cleanest office on the first two floors of the building. Jim Runyan.

On August 7, radio station WHB told the nation that the stockyards were open, and Armour & Company resumed slaughtering cattle. However, the Cudahy Packing Co. decision to close its plant meant a loss of 1800 jobs and a multimillion dollar annual payroll. In time the other packing houses would follow suit.

The resumption of one stockyard activity was noted in an August 13, 1951 story by the Star:

> "The reopening of the sheep market at the stockyards became official at 7:10 last night when George, a lamb with a face as black as coal, trotted into a pen from a truck. The 5-month-old lamb was raised on a bottle by Dickie Lentz, 8, a son of Mr. and Mrs. D.S. Lentz of Paola, Kansas."

After the flood, the two banks serving the stockyards found new homes. Interstate National Bank carried on its business activities at the First National Bank, and Stockyards National Bank moved its operations to Commerce Bank where its assets were liquidated, with Commerce Trust Company absorbing the bank, its officers and employees.

Flood control efforts resumed in earnest after 1951. After much bi-state cooperation among politicians from both parties and with the aid of the Corps of Engineers, there emerged today's massive protective program of locks, reservoirs, levees and lakes that has removed the majority of the West Bottoms from the 100-year flood plain...it now lies within a 500-year flood plain.

Following the 1951 flood, Joyce C. Hall, Hallmark Cards founder, commissioned Norman Rockwell to paint "The Spirit of Kansas City" portraying "the resiliency to come together and rebuild." The Kansas City Spirit, supra.

COWTOWN

Cattle Trails And West Bottom Tales

Photo courtesy of Hallmark Cards

Thomas Hart Benton also depicted the flood in "Flood Disaster", which in lithograph form was sent to each member of Congress to encourage passage of a flood relief appropriations bill during the 1951 legislative session.

C O W T O W N

Cattle Trails And West Bottom Tales

Marooned!

Flood destruction everywhere
Photos courtesy Blueprint for Disaster!

124

COWTOWN

Cattle Trails And West Bottom Tales

TWO STOCKYARD VISITORS OF NOTE

In 1953, Kansas City entertained a visit by the most heralded warrior from Abilene, Kansas since Wild Bill Hickok...President Dwight D. Eisenhower. It had been 54 years since the National Hereford Cattle Show had ushered in the American Royal. The President, accompanied by Agriculture Secretary Ezra Taft Benson, came to dedicate the new American Hereford Association building with its Hereford bull looking down on the West Bottoms and the stockyards. An inscription on the bull's pedestal celebrated the faith of the pioneers and the determination of those who had established Herefords as leaders in the beef cattle world.

Hereford Bull on pedestal
Noll Postcard Collection

COWTOWN

Cattle Trails And West Bottom Tales

Fred Olander (left) took advantage of the opportunity to get the Secretary on a horse for a look around the stockyards.

Photo courtesy of Mina Olander Steen per Elmwood book

Ike also attended a performance of the American Royal. When he entered the building in the company of his host Harry Darby, Jay Dillingham and a Secret Service escort, John Dillingham tagged along, part of a large crowd that had undergone no security check whatsoever. When the Secret Service agents asked the Senator who was in charge of security, Darby pointed to Jay and said "He is." John still remembers with admiration his father's aplomb at the sudden appointment and accompanying responsibility. He also remembers the grandeur of the occasion:

> "In 1953, it was an honor and great pleasure for me to see President Dwight Eisenhower, guest of Senator Harry Darby, at the opening performance of the American Royal. What a sight in that darkened old Royal building to see the arena filled with Hereford cattle, each with two handlers in long white jackets under the bright lights, and to hear 'Hail to the Chief and see the President of the United State enter the show ring." Charles N. Kimball Lecture, supra, by John Dillingham.

****

A November, 1955 visit to Kansas City by former Dominican Republic president Rafael Leonidas Trujillo was largely a shopping expedition by the generalissimo and his entourage of fourteen. Preparations included establishing a Commerce Trust bank account. In addition to acquiring horses to be shipped home, there was a trip to Shipley's. According to the Kansas City Star's Joe Roberts: "At the Charles P. Shipley Saddlery and Mercantile Company, the general and his son purchased a dozen cowboy hats, three dozen blankets, a dozen lariats, riding boots and saddles." He also bought Herbert Woolf's prize-winning black stallion Saxony.

Trujillo's Kansas City tour included visits to packing houses and a reception for 700 guests at the Hotel Muehlbach where the guest list included stockyard personages.

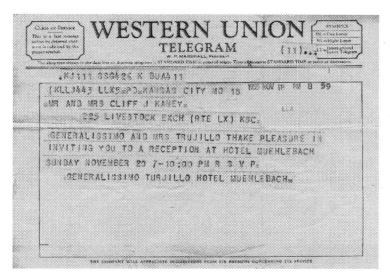

Telegram courtesy of Sally Ruddy

COWTOWN

Cattle Trails And West Bottom Tales

WARM MEMORIES

Soon after joining his father at Swift & Henry, 19-year-old Jim Runyan and his friend Tom Spencer had an experience reminiscent of an earlier time in the West Bottoms.

"The Stockyards Hotel was across the street from the horse barn. The second story of the hotel was even with the roof of the horse barn.

"One hot summer day, Tom Spencer and I were hanging out in the horse barn when we heard loud laughing and shouting from the second story of the hotel. The hotel did not have any air conditioning and the big hall windows facing Genesee Street were wide open.

"Tom and I got up on the roof of the barn. We could see in the hotel windows and there was Big Alice frolicking in the hall-way with several of her cowboy friends. The weather was hot so they didn't have any clothes on! What entertainment for a couple of 19 year old boys."

For cowboys or yard men, stockyards work was over for the week by Wednesday afternoon when all the cattle had been sold. With four bars on Genessee Street and several on Wyoming, there was a lot of drinking and dancing until early on the following Monday morning. Railroad employees waiting in the West End Bar for the trip west allowed occasional revelers to sleep it off in an empty cattle car. Jim Runyan reported that on more than one occasion the nappers woke up in Topeka.

Jim also recalled the brief tenure at Swift & Henry of another youngster, a "smart Alec":

"One summer in the mid-50s, Mr. Kaney hired a young man and put him to work in the fat cattle alley. The alley had 4 or 6 pens on each side and when the salesman sold all the cattle, he would have one man set the gates to the scale and then turn out one pen at a time with a yard man in between to keep the cattle separated. It was important that they not be mixed because they had different owners and different prices.

"They turned out a load behind the new boy. The cattle got a little close and Mr. Kaney hollered 'watch your ass'! The new kid dropped his pants and looked behind. He didn't last long."

* * * * * * * * * * * * * * * * * *

As a teen-ager, Saint Luke's Hospital CEO G. Richard Hastings (now retired) looked forward to his stockyard visits with his father. They brought cattle from the family farm, and Rich kept an eye on them during the trip. Once a train derailment in the middle of Oklahoma necessitated an impromptu cattle roundup, but their 100 steers were located and resumed their journey little the worse for wear.

COWTOWN

Cattle Trails And West Bottom Tales

****

Stockyard historian Alan Rogers first began to visit the stockyards with his father, a cattle buyer, in 1958, at the age of 7.

"I remember investigating the Exchange Building, going from floor to floor, looking around and peeking in offices, at which time long-established commission firms still had old mounted sets of steer horns hanging on their walls. On one occasion, I was up on Nine (as some yardmen used to say) and wandered down to the Exchange Hall, a Stockyard Co. meeting room, Room 905, a door that was usually locked but for some reason that day, it wasn't. I stepped inside and saw, for the first time, the Yard Company's collection of old mounted steer horns, which included elk antlers, buffalo horns and deer antlers. They were scattered about and many of them were hanging from the support pillars. It had a lasting impact, and it was from my time spent in the Exchange Building that my lifelong interest in the horns of Texas cattle began."

Alan has the finest collection of antique cattle long horns in the United States. Many of them have a history, beginning with the days of the trail drives. In Alan's National Texas Longhorn Museum, a website dedicated to the study of the horns of Texas cattle, this specimen is described:

"Longhorn steer shipped by rail to Kansas City in 1924. Placed in the quarantine section to inspect for tick fever. An old, mature steer, perhaps 15 years old. Weighed 710 pounds. Sold for 6 cents a pound to the Cudahy Packing Co. where he was killed by the hammer. Horns hung in the office of Cassidy Southeastern Commission Co. from 1924 — 1972, a firm for whom my Dad bought cattle. 4 feet 9 inches tip to tip. One of the classic early day Longhorn shapes."

The largest piece of horn furniture, a dresser displayed at the 1904 World's Fair in St. Louis (from National Texas Longhorn Museum)

129

COWTOWN

Cattle Trails And West Bottom Tales

****

George Sanders was the same age as Alan Rogers when he made his acquaintance with the stockyards. He later (November 28, 2010) reminisced for the Kansas City Star Magazine:

"I was 7 years old when a friend and I, along with my chameleon Sneaky, ran away from home to be cowboys in the stockyards in the West Bottoms. Later I worked there every summer with my father, a cattle broker.

"Mondays were busiest, with more than 50,000 head of cattle arriving. It was the late 1950s and Dad had pens in Bull Alley on the north end. I was in charge of the water and hay. Horses pulling wagons delivered hay, and the guys pitched it into the pens.

"The Leavenworth penitentiary and a chain of drive-in restaurants were Dad's clients. The prisons bought the best cattle. The drive-ins (no longer in business) bought the cheapest, sickest and worst cows.

"The alleys between the pens were lined with bricks laid on their sides. On top was a mixture of hay, manure and urine. Rich buyers like Syl Metzger rode horses; he gave me shiny 50-cent pieces and always smoked big cigars.

"A short train ran between sections of pens, and I rode on the engine a lot. I often found pig tusks, from which I made a necklace by drilling holes and stringing them on raw hide. The Kansas River was west of the yards. I liked to go there to throw rocks at large rats.

"Outside the Livestock Exchange Building was a boot scrape and a water trough with brushes to wash manure off boots before entering. Inside were offices with rolltop desks, meeting rooms lined with racks of mounted cattle horns, a bank, barbershop, post office and cafeteria. Hot roast beef sandwiches were the best. Tommy Gilmore's concession stand sold pop, candy and cigarettes. The elevator operator was a well-dressed Hispanic fellow with not a hair out of place.

"I frequently visited the baker, who often gave me a piece of pie or a doughnut. I remember seeing him sweep up flour from the floor, sift it and put it back in the bin."

****

Many city-dwelling youngsters visiting the stockyards learned some of the basics there. Charlotte Wornall Kirk attended a West Bottoms stock show with her grandfather, Eli Wheat, a cattleman from Camden Point, Missouri. There he pointed out the part of the steer that produced the brisket, her favorite cut of meat, and explained how to identify the steer with the best brisket.

130

COWTOWN

Cattle Trails And West Bottom Tales

****

A Saturday horseback ride in the stockyards was an occasional treat for teen-ager Mary Shaw (Shawsie) Branton of nearby Independence, Missouri. Thanks to a neighbor she was permitted to ride in the empty stockyard alleys, where the clatter of her horse's hooves on the brick floors was an unforgettable sound.

****

In his book "Dust to Destiny — It's Just the Cowboy in Me", AuthorHouse 2011, Walt Krier included a chapter entitled "Stockyards and Cowboys" which recalls in part: "Cowboys and stockyards were many a young man's dream and I was one cowboy who was hooked. When I was about six years old my dad would lift me in the saddle and I was expected to bring up the drag, or slow cattle. We drove fat cattle to Olpe, Kansas railroad pens to be shipped to Kansas City, Missouri stockyards to be sold and then slaughtered, by one of the three packing houses located across the river from the Kansas City, Missouri stockyards.

"Dad would bring his suitcase as he had a free ride in the train caboose car...

"Later, when Dad was shipping cattle from Kansas to Missouri and it is time for him to make his way back to Englewood, Kansas, he must first stop at the Stockyard Bank to collect for his cattle and then have a first class dinner at the Golden Ox Restaurant, in Kansas City, Missouri, and purchase a few fifths of whiskey for the cowboys at home."

****

Mark Flaherty grew up on a family farm in Kansas, some 80 miles from Kansas City. The family raised cattle and pigs, primarily for consumption at home. But once or twice a year there were "extras", to be trucked to the livestock market in Kansas City. Mark began to make these trips at age nine, with his father and older brother. They were exciting.

These were the mid-fifties, and by this time a large number of farmers from small farms were making the same trip. Mark well remembers the big traffic jams of trucks entering and exiting the stockyards.

Upon entering the yards, the loaded Flaherty truck was driven across a scale and the weight recorded, then driven to the pen of their broker or commission agent and unloaded. The empty truck was then driven across the scale again and the change in weight recorded to establish the sale price of the entire load of livestock.

Mark watched from the alley beside the pen as the broker and a packing house buyer negotiated a price per hundred-weight (100 pounds). They then went to the broker's small office in the Livestock Exchange Building and received payment. Part of the payment was in cash, and Mark and his brother

Cattle Trails And West Bottom Tales

went downstairs with their father to the wonderful Golden Ox restaurant for a meal. The food was "fantastic." The Flahertys then climbed into their empty truck and went home.

Young Mark loved those trips to the stockyards in Kansas City.

There were also visits to the American Royal, where they showed their livestock. These trips afforded more time to look around, although there were no Folly Theater visits for the youngsters. On at least one occasion, an older cousin asked Mark, then age six, to exhibit his pigs in the show ring and they "won all the prizes." Mark believes that the young age of the handler contributed to the result.

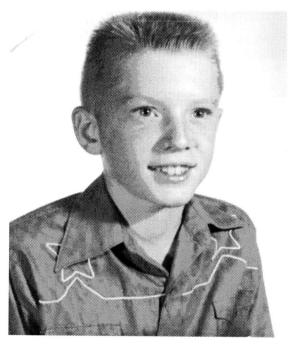

Mark Flaherty, at age 11
Photo courtesy of Mark Flaherty

Mark attended Auburn High School in Kansas, along with the eleven other farm kids who started with him as freshmen in 1962. He was drafted in to the US Army in 1969, where he served one tour in Viet Nam as a paratrooper with an airborne infantry unit. He was wounded twice and ended his service as a decorated staff sergeant. He finished college and law school and is engaged in the private practice of law. He started law school in 1975, where he was an editor of the Law Review. He's been engaged in the private practice of law since he graduated in 1978.

COWTOWN

Cattle Trails And West Bottom Tales

LOULA LONG COMBS

In her centennial history of the American Royal, Heather Paxton noted that the American Royal show in 1960 saw the end of an era when Loula Long Combs rode in her last Royal. The daughter of lumber baron Robert A. Long, Loula Long had exercised the family horses near their majestic Corinthian Hall home (now the Kansas City Museum) before making the move to spacious Longview Farm in Lee's Summit, Missouri.

The horse barn at Longview Farm, beautifully restored, became an elementary school in the Lee's Summit School District. The 100-year-old horse show arena is the school gymnasium. The school library has a reading room that was once a horse stall. And the hallways are named after Loula's horses.

From the very first of the American Royal years, Mrs. Combs was the star of the show. Her stable of high stepping hackney ponies hitched to signature 2-wheel carts called roadsters were crowd pleasers — a George IV Phaeton roadster was her favorite. She drove around the arena with one or two of her Boston Bull terriers on the seat beside her. She was the only lady in the ring, competing with several gentlemen drivers. Splendid hats, some of them inherited from her mother, Mrs. R.A. Long, were a part of the elegant picture she made… Barnum & Bailey asked her to go on tour with their circus.

Customarily, Mrs. Combs would arrive early. The ushers, often young women who lived on Strawberry Hill, also arrived early and gathered at her box where she would pin a corsage of roses from her Longview Farm on each girl.

Loula Long Combs at home, Longview Farm
Photo courtesy of The American Royal

133

She was accompanied in her box by her two trainers. It was her practice to watch the crowd and, if she saw a family with children standing by the rail, to dispatch a trainer to ask if they had seats; if not, they were offered seats in the box.

Sally Ruddy was in the audience the night of Loula's last ride:

> "The elegant lady drove into the ring with her dog on the seat beside her. The organ music stopped and the huge crowd was silent. They rose to their feet and stood quietly as she drove past...a respectful tribute to a lovely lady." Sally Ruddy.

A Loula Long carriage is exhibited at the American Royal Museum,
together with some of her prize ribbons and trophies

Steve Noll Photo

COWTOWN

Cattle Trails And West Bottom Tales

TIME RUNS OUT

In 1967, Armour closed its Kansas City plant, one of the last packers to go. But the cattlemen continued to buy and sell.

In 1969, some of the old cattle pens were torn down to make way for a new public auction building. Auction sales were preferable to the traditional trading "on the bricks" where one man might be the only bidder on a load of cattle. Now a barn full of people could compete. Producers might still consign cattle to commission firms for sale by private transactions ("treaties"), but more often now the sales would be public spectacles. Seated buyers and sellers could watch in air conditioned comfort as cattle were brought in and the auctioneer kept up a steady chant while buyers bid on the animals they wanted to buy.

Among those who offered cattle for sale at auction were the proprietors of the Richard Robbins Anchor D Ranch, in Belvedere, Kansas. According to Paul McKie of Tonganoxie's Tailgate Ranch, Robbins was a valued customer of Fred Olander and, whenever the Robbins' Hereford calves were on the auction block, the dignified Olander could be counted on to rise to his feet and give his "dollar a hundred" speech. His message included a description of the virtues of the Robbins family and their ranch, and the high quality of their livestock. He was very convincing in his blue suit and vest, his "downtown" fedora hat, and his shock of white hair, and the result was inevitably a bid of $1 dollar per hundred-weight (pounds) above the prevailing bid price. Auction regulars had heard it all before but looked forward to it anyway.

In a group picture of an auction crowd, Jay Dillingham (center row) in his Stetson smiles at the camera while Fred Olander in his "downtown" hat, two rows back, prepares his "dollar a hundred" speech.

Photo courtesy of Wilborn & Fitzgerald

135

COWTOWN

Cattle Trails And West Bottom Tales

The Kansas City Star Magazine reported that auctioneer Hugh Morehead attributed his durable voice to "drinking good whiskey and breathing night air." He gave up smoking when he started to develop a little voice trouble, substituting a chaw that he disposed of fastidiously in a wastebasket. His was an important role.

George Morse, a Missouri native, was a Kansas City Stockyards auctioneer with star power. In 1972, the American Hereford Association bestowed on him the title of "Master Salesman." And he received from John Wayne an annual invitation to preside over the sale of Wayne's breeding stock at his Arizona ranch.

According to Morse, the ideal auction chant is clear, rhythmic and continuous.

Ray Sims, a stockyards auction veteran from Raymore, Missouri, is on the Saddle & Sirloin Wall of Fame. He is credited with accelerating the pace of the auction chant, resulting in more sales transactions.

The Kansas City Star reported the retirement of Muggins Hall of Van Buren, Arkansas after 64 years of bringing cattle to the stockyards. His experience as he roamed the Ozark hills on horseback was convivial...each transaction sealed with a swig of moonshine provided by the seller. Then, aided by several coon hounds, Muggins drove the cattle to a railroad and loaded them aboard cattle cars for the two-day trip to Kansas City.

****

The last tenant left the Stockyards Hotel in October 1969. The demise of the 3-story hotel left the West End as the only hotel in the stockyards district.

The remnants of the West End Hotel, 1629 Genessee.
Steve Noll Photo

COWTOWN

Cattle Trails And West Bottom Tales

The west side of the 1600 block on Genessee is the site of the Livestock Exchange Building. Across the street at 1611 were located Haggard's Locker Room, Billiard parlor and Shoe Shine parlor. That building still stands but the Haggard enterprises are gone – as are the livestock men who were their customers. Further south, at 1615 Genessee, was the Genessee Bar – also gone, along with its rowdy cowboy patrons. And at the end of the block, 1629, stands the Shipley building.

In 1972, after 67 years in the saddlery business, Shipley closed its doors.
The Shipley building, built to last, still stands.

Steve Noll photo.

COWTOWN

Cattle Trails And West Bottom Tales

R. CROSBY KEMPER JR.

William Thornton Kemper was a shareholder and director of one of the pioneer stockyard banks, the Stock Yards National. His son, R. (Rufus) Crosby Kemper Sr., also a banker, was for many years treasurer of the American Royal and declined its presidency more than once. Shortly after his father's death, R. Crosby Kemper Jr. announced that the Kemper family would give $1.5 million to the American Royal. This launched events that resulted in the Royal's Kemper Arena. Heather Paxton, supra.

The birth of the Kemper Arena was preceded by some serious labor pains, principally a conflict over its West Bottoms location. The American Royal building, on Kansas City Stockyards Company land, had deteriorated over the years. There were those who thought that a new image for Kansas City should replace the cowtown of yore, and that a new sports arena and an exposition building housing the American Royal should be built elsewhere.

Banker Crosby Kemper Jr. was a vehement historic preservationist of Kansas City's Western roots and heritage; his frequent contacts with correspondent bankers throughout the mid-West convinced him that the storied cowtown past was also part of Kansas City's future. Consequently he favored a continued West Bottoms location for the Royal and its Arena, and increased the Kemper donation to $3.2 million for such a project. The Royal Board of Governors followed with a vote to exercise its option to buy the site from the Kansas City Stockyards Company. An additional $2.7 million was raised in a campaign, and the City Council agreed to issue $5.6 million in general obligation bonds underwritten by investment banker Stern Brothers.

Kemper Arena
Noll Postcard Collection

There were other glitches but finally everything came together in the 17,000 seat R. Crosby Kemper Sr. Memorial Arena at 17th and Genessee. At the October 18, 1974 dedication, Secretary of Agriculture Earl Butz recognized the American Royal as "a major connecting link between the city's trade and transportation facilities and the agricultural empire that surrounds them." Heather Paxton, supra.

When the Republican National Convention convened in Kansas City in July 1976, it met in the Kemper Arena. Crosby Kemper Jr. opened the proceedings and then presented to the Convention chairman a gavel made of Missouri walnut.

For the next thirty years, "the Kemper" would serve as the city's primary venue for indoor sports, concerts, and other big events.

R. Crosby Kemper Jr. was an honorary chairman of the American Royal Centennial in 1999.

R. Crosby Kemper Jr. was convinced that Kansas City's
storied cowtown past was also part of its future.

Photo courtesy of UMB Bank

C O W T O W N

Cattle Trails And West Bottom Tales

POSSUM TROT AND BARBECUE

A September 12, 1977 story in the Kansas City Star by financial writer Wendell Cochran reported "wide agreement in the Kansas City agricultural community that within a few years the Kansas City Stockyards no longer will be operating."

In 1978, the owner of the Genessee Inn described it as a neighborhood inn without a neighborhood. The days of whooping cowboys riding their horses through the bars were gone and would never come back. Gone also were colorful characters such as "Racehorse" McMorrow, so called because he used to make runs to an Omaha, Nebraska racetrack with bets on horses. While many of the hands still worked on horseback, others suffered the indignity of riding motor scooters. The Star's Jim Lapham described the plight of the motorized wrangler:

> "I'm an old cowhand, West of Twelfth and Grand And my legs ain't bowed cause all I ever rode, Was a dang blasted puttity putt putt motorcycle An the fust man laughs I'll hit him right in the mouth."

Now they ride off on Ol' Putt.
Kansas City Star Photo

COWTOWN

Cattle Trails And West Bottom Tales

****

In 1979, the Historic Kansas City Foundation brought the Possum Trot festival to the West Bottoms, to a site at 10th and Genessee. The front page of the Possum Trot Gazette featured a historic picture of Union Avenue, with horse-drawn vehicles and the Blossom House.

Possum Trot Gazette photo courtesy of Historic Kansas City Foundation

Possum Trot was a celebration organized in 1974 by the Foundation and the Kansas City Missouri Junior League and named for the settlement that became Kansas City. The "Possum Trot" name was rejected by the city fathers in favor of commemorating the area's Kansa Indians with "Town of Kansas." "Town of Kansas" became "Kansas City"; the name was officially changed in 1889. A Short History of Possum Trot, 1974 - 1986, David W. Jackson, archivist, Jackson County Historical Society.

A 1977 Gazette group picture of Possum Trot participants, labeled "A Nite in Old Possum Trot", included future Kansas City, Missouri mayors Richard Berkley and Kay Waldo, Kansas City Chiefs' NFL Hall of Famer Jan Stenerud, Squire Publisher Tom Leathers, civic leaders Alvin Brooks, Joan Dillon, Muriel Kauffman, and Jerry Smith, Historic Kansas City Foundation president Day Kerr and event chair Linda Cook.

COWTOWN

Cattle Trails And West Bottom Tales

Kay Waldo
Alvin Brooks
Rosemary Smithson
Jan Stenrud
Joan Dillon
Muriel Kauffman
Don Meyer
Nancy Palmer

Jerry Smith
Linda Bryan
Tom Leathers
Hal Sandy
Linda Cook
Day Kerr
Richard Berkley

Possum Trot Festival participants included celebrities and civic leaders.
Photo courtesy of Historic Kansas City Foundation

Former Kansas City mayor and former acting sheriff of Possum Trot (1977) Charles B. Wheeler received the 1979 Possum Trot Award for helping save and restore historic landmarks.

Possum Trot was repeated at the stockyards site in 1980, 1981 and 1982, offering wooden nickels, a special commemorative postmark, and toe tappin', knee slappin' music.

****

The Kemper Arena roof collapsed in 1979, under the strain of torrential rain and 70 miles per hour winds. Pending repairs, the next Royal was held in the old American Royal facility. Heather Paxton, supra, quotes Robert Hovey, the American Royal president at the time:

> "We got to have the show in the old arena, the area where I had grown up with the American Royal, with the walk around and the boxes. My wife and I sat in the President's Box, which was in the center on one side. We knew it was the last time."

****

The American Royal Bar-B-Q contest (known as The Royal) had its beginning the following year, at the urging of Bob Hovey. The Golden Ox provided the site and electricity for the dueling contenders, free of charge. The contest has grown to be the largest such event in the world...100,000 fans watch 550 teams go at it across 22 acres in the West Bottoms...the World Series of Barbecue.

COWTOWN

Cattle Trails And West Bottom Tales

Prior to the Civil War, most African-Americans visiting the West Bottoms came by way of the historic Underground Railroad, fleeing slaves on their way to the Free State of Kansas. Their route through the bottoms is traced by the Freedom Trail, part of the Riverfront Heritage Trail. The Exodus Family, a sculpture at 8th and Belleview by Edward "Muskogee" Hogan, depicts the slave exodus as the "exodusters" attempt to cross the West Bottoms.

In the years following emancipation, freed slaves migrated to Kansas City and the West Bottoms, attracted by jobs in stockyards and slaughterhouses. They brought along their BBQ skills. Near the century's end, another great migration occurred: Texas cattle.

Doug Worgul added, in his "The Grand Barbecue, supra:

> "The confluence of rivers and railroads in Kansas City was another major determinant in our becoming a barbecue capital. In the 19th century, buyers and sellers used the riversand railroads to transport livestock in and out of Kansas City and a thriving meatpacking industry developed. The ready availability of cheap meat and the abundance of hardwood trees with which this area has also been blessed, provided barbecuers with the two fundamental necessities of their craft.

> "But it was the migration of African-Americans to the region, between 1879 and 1881, and then again in the 20th century, that was the single most important factor in barbecue becoming such a distinct part of Kansas City culture."

THE END

In April of 1984, when it appeared that sale and closure of the yards was imminent, Ray Davis "rounded up 17 friends and bought the place." Kansas City Star, September 29, 1985. Ownership of the Kansas City stockyards transferred from Kansas City Stock Yards Co. of Maine to Kansas City Stockyards Co. in a ceremony in the area behind the Livestock Exchange Building. The new owners had a vested interest in the livestock business - a disparate group that included the owner of the Livestock Exchange Building, the general manager of the Golden Ox, the Swift & Henry Order Buying Company, and auctioneer Hugh Morehead. The transaction occurred on a regular Thursday cattle auction day; businessmen in pin stripes and ties and weather beaten auction regulars watched as Kansas City, Missouri Mayor Richard Berkley outbid Kansas City, Kansas Mayor Jack Reardon, for a shipment of feeder cattle.

Kansas City Stockyards Co. investors announced their intent to continue to operate and improve the services and facilities of the stockyards. Ray Davis, now company president, commented: "I don't say it will last forever. It will last as long as I have anything to say about it."

The big packing houses were gone, however. Livestock still arrived at the stockyards but after sale they were shipped to smaller, modern packing plants elsewhere. Swift & Henry cattle were sent via Union Pacific to Monfort of Colorado, Inc., packers in Greeley, Colorado. According to stockyards historian Edmonds P. (Bud) Mackey, the industry evolved into a modernized business with decentralization of function and without the burden of antiquated packing plants.

A January 1988 article by the Star's agribusiness editor noted that although activity had slowed in Kansas City's livestock marketing, the stockyards had survived as well as their legends. But in the ensuing three years, empty pens were a common sight. Gone were the bellowing cattle, the shouting yardmen, the banging gates, and the distinctive aroma. Missing too were the members of the stockyards fraternity: "The laughing and shouting and the horseplay and the jokes are long since gone from Genessee Street." The Stockyard Shaman

The FFA moved to Louisville, Kentucky after the organization's 1988 convention. The welcome annual invasion by blue-jacketed future farmers would be missed, but R. Crosby Kemper Jr. organized a worthy replacement: the AFA (Agriculture Future of America). The initial organizational meetings were conducted at the farm of Alexander (Sandy) Kemper, Crosby's son and later the chairman of the AFA board of directors. Mark Flaherty was asked by Crosby to assist in organizing the AFA; he became a big supporter in what he considered to be a "wonderful program" and helped identify corporate sponsors to provide summer internships and college scholarships for participants.

Only three years later, September 26, 1991, the last cattle auction was held in the stockyards. The Kansas City stockyards then closed their doors and ceased to exist. Michael J. Satchell wrote in the Kansas City Star:

COWTOWN

Cattle Trails And West Bottom Tales

"From longhorns to shorthorns to no horns at all, the pens have swung open and the final gates closed on a grunting, bawling, bleating, squealing herd 443 million strong, and if there's a livestock heaven the Kansas City stockyards are not fondly remembered.

"This town was launched on a shuffling tide of T-bone, rib-eye, sausage, hamburger and loin chop on the hoof that brought wealth to the area and fixed its western image."

On October 5, the final dismantling of the stockyards began, with auctioneers selling off everything. Buyers were urged to buy a piece of Kansas City history, and they did...hay wagons, branding irons, high back saddles, and even a 22-year-old quarter horse named Baldy. Paving bricks from the stockyards grace many Kansas City patios, where a faint aroma after a rainstorm is a reminder of their origin.

The opening paragraph of Rise and Fall of a Cowtown (Kansas City Star Magazine, December 9, 2012) by Rick Montgomery reads as follows:

"In the 1990s, local historians and labor groups, arranging a bus tour of important industrial sites, scoured Kansas City's West Bottoms for whatever remained of the meatpacking giants that grew the city.

"Not a smokestack. Not an employee parking sign. Not a whiff of odor."

The Armour name survives, however, and it is everywhere...Armour Boulevard, the Armour Hills and Armour Fields neighborhoods, the A(Armour)SB Bridge, Kansas City, Kansas's Armourdale and North Kansas City's Armour Road. The Armours' mansions are gone (one teardown was replaced for a time by the Gayety Theatre burlesque house), but the Armour farm home still stands at 6740 Pennsylvania. And several Armours are interred in Kansas City, Missouri's Elmwood Cemetery, where the Armour Chapel is a memorial to Kirkland Armour, erected by his widow Annie.

The Livestock Exchange Building also survives, the last vestige of the stockyards, very much alive and occupied by an eclectic group of tenants.

COWTOWN

Cattle Trails And West Bottom Tales

LEGACIES

The American Royal's economic impact on the Kansas City area continues to be significant, and in addition to the World Series of Barbeque it annually hosts some of the Midwest's largest livestock expositions, professional rodeos accompanied by the country's top country music entertainers, and prestigious horse shows including an Arabian Horse Show and the National Championship Saddlebred Horse Competition.

Another stockyards legacy is mid-America's burgeoning animal health industry.

Animals are disease prone and easily injured. The bumping and rolling of cattle cars bound for Kansas City's stockyards knocked down the weaker animals and the long sharp horns of range cattle gouged flesh. Once at the stockyards, they might be subjected to fire or flood or the occasional major winter storm. The blizzard of 1886 killed hundreds of head by burying them in snow or subjecting them to temperatures of 28 degrees below zero. All of that livestock living in close quarters generated a need for veterinarians, and the animal doctors were followed by animal health care companies. Kansas City Business Magazine, May 2013, Dana Macan, Group Publisher.

Kansas City Veterinary College
Noll Postcard collection

In 1891 the Kansas City Veterinary College was founded with three students and two rented rooms. Enrollment quickly increased and by 1908 it had become the largest veterinary school in the country. It produced doctors of veterinary science until 1918. Today the area is served by top-notch successors, the veterinary medicine schools at Kansas State University and the University of Missouri.

COWTOWN

Cattle Trails And West Bottom Tales

The Kansas City Veterinary College graduated 1,857 doctors of veterinary medicine and science in its time. It wasn't all work and no play; there were student football teams, a glee club, and a 16-piece brass band. Some of the graduates founded serum companies and other animal health products. One was involved in the eradication of Texas fever, and another in the treatment of hoof and mouth disease in Mexico.

The last class, of 1918, included the Loveless family quartette (Harmon, Herman, Lela and Lola Loveless) from Modesto, California. While in school they lived together in a 7-bedroom house and had a joint bank account. They performed on the Chautauqua Circuit and appeared on the Groucho Marx, Herb Schreiner, and To Tell the Truth programs. (Kansas City Veterinary College 1891-1918; The Foundation of the Kansas City Animal Health Corridor. Howard H. Erickson, D. V. M, PhD.)

Photo from University of Iowa Libraries, copy courtesy of Howard H. Erickson, DVM, Phd.

Dr. Anita Eagle Frevert, supra, reports that six of the eleven sons of family patriarchs Alec and Jack Eagle enrolled in the Kansas City Veterinary College, their packing house employment experience having convinced them that meat inspection was preferable to following the family butcher trade. "Ruthless labor practices turned the once-respected butcher trade into just another hand on the disassembly line." Rick Montgomery, supra.

One son, Robert, was a tackle on the College football team, and William was a quarterback. A cousin, Alexander, played center, and a son-in-law, Robert Grimes, was the left end. After graduation, Robert Grimes and William Eagle became federal veterinarians along with three other sons of Alec and two cousins, Jack Eagle's sons. All worked for the U.S. Department of

COWTOWN

Cattle Trails And West Bottom Tales

Agriculture's Bureau of Animal Industry (B.A.I.) inspecting packing house meat and stockyards, and eradicating cattle and hog diseases on farms and ranches.

In 1901, following his graduation from the Kansas City Veterinary College, one of Alec's sons, Richard, arrived at Port Elizabeth, South Africa on his 21st birthday with a British Army captain's commission and a shipload of Missouri mules and horses for British Boer War soldiers. He later wrote a textbook on Meat Hygiene and Pathology at the University of Chicago where he taught.

Richard's brother, Thomas, was B.A.I inspector for Missouri and Kansas and officed in the Livestock Exchange building. In 1913 Thomas Eagle, together with six brothers and cousins sitting around a kitchen table, founded Eagle Laboratories, followed by Eagle Biological and Supply Co. and Eagle Anti-Cholera Serum.

In 1917, Thomas Eagle was one of eight veterinarians invited to Washington D.C. to plan a campaign to eliminate hoof and mouth disease in cattle. B.A.I. Director Dr. John R. Mohler, a 1901 graduate of the Kansas City Veterinary College, joined them there.

Mules were used to transport essential supplies across the "Hump" (Himalayan Mountains) to the Chinese Army in World War II. The oldest son of Thomas, Lt. Col. Thomas McCauley Eagle, was the U.S. Cavalry (Veterinary Corps) officer who supplied those pack animals. He was also involved in disposing of horses as they were replaced by armored corps vehicles and jeeps. After his Army discharge in 1945, he founded the Eagle Animal Hospital in Riverside, Missouri, downstream from the Kansas City stockyards. In addition, he wrote a syndicated column, "Pet Doctor" and was an associate professor at the M.U. School of Veterinary Medicine in Columbia.

****

In 2013, KC Business Magazine, supra, reported that the Kansas City area's biosciences industry fostered an animal health sector, still growing, and a redefinition of the city's "cowtown" image. And the Kansas City Area Life Sciences Institute, abetted by Jim Spigarelli and the Midwest Research Institute, helped formalize the animal health corridor concept. Ingram's Magazine.

Geographically, the sector lies between the cities of Columbia and St. Joseph in Missouri and Manhattan, Kansas. John Dillingham refers to the area as "the Silicon Valley" of agriculture. It is the butcher, grain miller, and distributor of the Missouri Valley and hosts the world's largest concentration of animal health industry assets. In addition, it is the site of 32% of global sales by the animal health industry. K. C. Business Magazine, supra.

***********************.

Carl DiCapo, while national president of the National Agriculture Hall of Fame, championed a move by the Hall from nearby Bonner Springs, Kansas to the West Bottoms, to be closer to the American Royal complex.

COWTOWN

Cattle Trails And West Bottom Tales

The Saddle & Sirloin Club History, supra, reported that the Hall of Fame when proposed in 1959 was to be located in the Kansas City area thanks to a number of Club members including Senator Darby, Kansas City Star Editor Roy Roberts and Kansas City, Missouri Mayor H. Roe Bartle. A 1960 Star editorial stated that the Royal and the Hall supplemented each other and proximity would reinforce that relationship.

Chartered by the 86th Congress and signed into law by President Eisenhower in 1960, the Hall is dedicated to celebrating and communicating the heritage of America's farmers, while serving as the repository of the history and tradition of American agriculture. The 38 inductees of the Hall of Fame range from Squanto, the American Indian who showed the starving pilgrims how to plant maize using fish as fertilizer, to Senator Robert Dole who played a major role in the development and bipartisan passage of agricultural legislation during his long government service.

Senator Robert Dole   Squanto, The First Agricultural Agent

Hall of Fame Photos courtesy of Carl DiCapo

C O W T O W N

Cattle Trails And West Bottom Tales

WHAT'S NEXT?

Spawned by the stockyards the American Royal lives on there, thanks to a capital campaign headed by Malcolm (Mick) Aslin.

By 1987, the American Royal building was falling apart. Financing for a new building was achieved; R. Crosby Kemper Jr. worked closely with Mick Aslin, and James and Jonathan Kemper provided advance planning money from the William T. Kemper Fund. William Kemper had been an avid fan of the Royal, according to Heather Paxton. Other major donors included Joe and Joyce Hale (Arena Arena), the Sutherland family (Sutherland Exhibition Hall), Mr. and Mrs. Robert W. Wagstaff (Wagstaff Theatre), the I. A. O'Shaughnessy/Wysong Family Foundations, the Hall Family Foundation, and the Edith and Harry Darby Foundation. Many other individuals, companies and foundations gave monetary support…it was definitely a community effort. Heather Paxton.

The new complex opened in1992.

The Kemper Arena's prospects are diminished by the construction of the Sprint Center, uptown. The Kemper survives but UMB Bank CEO Mariner Kemper urges planning for a strong future of the West Bottoms by doing away with the Arena and rallying around those things that make Kansas City unique, such as the American Royal and its World Series of Barbeque. Other West Bottoms advocates favor retaining the Kemper Arena but converting it into a youth and amateur sports center.

****

William Haw foresees a more comprehensive future for the West Bottoms. He believes that proximity to the downtown core coupled with recreational use of the Kaw River frontage and Riverfront Heritage Trail can be the catalyst for unique community development incorporating residential, entertainment and commercial areas.

Haw, whose Haw Ranches are headquartered in the Livestock Exchange Building which he now owns, came to the West Bottoms about the time the stockyards shut down. He purchased the Exchange Building and painstakingly restored the interior including the distinctive floor tile pattern originally installed in 1908. He has also invested in other West Bottoms properties such as the historic, fully leased Drovers Telegram building with its Amigoni Urban Winery, and the popular Genesee Royale Bistro.

C O W T O W N

Cattle Trails And West Bottom Tales

Haw commissioned sculptor Robert Morris to create Bull Mountain. It is a form of land art replicating the cattle country of the Kansas Flint Hills, the beautiful blue stem pasturelands that supported thousands of transient, west Texas cattle, fattening before the end of their stockyard journey.

The bulls grazing on the "mountain" are the steel cutouts from Morris's spectacular sixteen-feet-tall Bull Wall sculpture at the American Royal complex.

The Robert Morris Bull Wall
Steve Noll Photos

151

COWTOWN

Cattle Trails And West Bottom Tales

The art is near the intersection of Genesee Street and the Dillingham Freeway Bridge
(Interstate 670)...the entrance to the Stockyards District

In his book Terminal Junction, Steven Dushan Milakov wrote of the intersection:

"There's no sign around telling us why this knot of land is where it is or what it is
intended to do. The answer I think is in its proximity to what's around it. It's the
entrance of the old stockyards area – the immigration point, mostly for cattle, but also
for pigs and other animals that completed their long rail journey on the Katy Railroad,
and who were all eventually herded to their collective fates inside the slaughter
houses. It was here where the cowboys, the dozens of wooden pens, the heavy, harsh
smell of animals, and the long cattle trains came together. It was the economy of the
times working in a fluid, systemic, and yes, deadly fashion." Published by Joe Vaughn
Associates, Prairie Village, Kansas, 2001

In the Haw Ranches office is a saddle given to Bill by an appreciative champion of his development
efforts. The donor told Haw that the previous owner of the saddle, father of the donor, had spent his
whole life in the stockyards and would want his saddle to have a home there. There is also in Haw's
office a large bronze sculpture of a cowboy on horseback, clad in a slicker with a coiled rope on his
saddle. One of his cowboys also rides the tiled second floor of the Livestock Exchange Building, in
the one-time lobby of the Livestock National Bank. A modest plaque on the lobby wall marks the
high water point of the 1951 flood.

C O W T O W N

Cattle Trails And West Bottom Tales

The Bill Haw Cowboy
Steve Noll Photo

****

Faultless Starch was a pioneer of the West. According to a company brochure:

"In the late 1890's, saleman John Nesbat took wagon loads of books into Texas and the Indian Territory and attached them to boxes of Faultless Starch with rubber bands. The books were designed to supplement or substitute for school texts, and many people learned to read using the 36 Faultless Starch Library books published from the 1890's to the 1930's. The books are still traded on auction web sites."

COWTOWN

Cattle Trails And West Bottom Tales

Today, the brochure notes, the Faultless West Bottoms plant "is located in the oldest section of Kansas City, Missouri, USA, which since Lewis & Clark has been regarded as an ideal commercial distribution point, being near the geographical center of North America; near the confluence of the Missouri River and the Kansas River, and served by the major rail lines and highways."

The original Faultless West Bottoms plant was a casualty of the infamous 1903 flood and later by the even more destructive 1951 catastrophe. It was the first company to rebuild.

In 1971, Faultless acquired Bon Ami and became Faultless Starch/Bon Ami.

After a 1998 general alarm fire in the abandoned Sunshine Biscuit factory across Eighth Street nearly engulfed the Faultless plant, the company opted to remain in the neighborhood where it had resided since 1887 rather than move to problem-free suburbia.

Situated at 1025 W. 8th Street, the Faultless/Bon Ami world headquarters office building is on the historic register and, together with its manufacturing plant and warehousing facility, is the linchpin of the Faultless 8th Street Campus Project. The Project is transforming a factory neighborhood north of the stockyards district. Faultless is no longer a lonesome enterprise surrounded by pock-marked streets and by crumbling buildings.

Steve Noll Photo

C O W T O W N

Cattle Trails And West Bottom Tales

OF JACKPOTS AND NUT FRIES

At lunch-time gatherings at the Golden Ox, retired stockyard cattle traders swap stories. They are a vanishing breed. The group often includes Jim Runyan, Gene Furnish, Ferd Good, Rudy Pinter, Alfred Neuberger, Ed Gorman, Wayne Theis, Norton Rixey, and Bob Bricker. The Hartford Insurance Company's Don Huebner occasionally joins them.

Rudy Pinter recalls his initiation as a green buyer of cattle for the Sambol Meat Packing Company, a small specialty packing house with strict size guidelines for purchases. His was on-the-job training at the hands of patient traders, who instructed instead of taking advantage of the neophyte. After young Rudy's repeated rejection of heifers and steers offered by Maxwell & Furnish as too large or too small to meet company guidelines, a good-natured Ben Furnish told him to "get the hell out" because "this is not a shoe store where you can order a size 7 1/8."

The Sambol Company made use of a lead cow, a decoy or "Judas" animal trained to lead a funeral procession of cattle from the stockyards to the packing houses. There they were placed in the "knocking" pen where they were killed by a sledge hammer blow to the head. The valuable lead cow was always carefully isolated in a separate pen. However, one day a zealous packing house employee moved the prized animal to the knocking pen, and she became just another side of beef on the conveyor line. "That was the end of our lead cow." Rudy well remembered the uproar over the loss of the lead cow.

Anecdotes reflect the earthy humor that prevailed in the pens and alleys of the stockyards. All recall the latter day Christmas Parties at the Hoof & Horn Club, always popular occasions. It was no longer the sedate organization governed by posted rules and described by the Star's Howard Turtle in his 1946 article. Yuletide festivities attracted many a grizzled stockyards veteran. Everyone remembered one such celebration attended by a cattle trader clad in his usual off-therack thrift shop attire. His wife had gone to a great deal of trouble in selecting her fashionable wardrobe for the event and it included some form-fitting black leather pants. When complimented on his wife's outfit, he responded: "If she ever farts, she'll blow her shoes off."

Another Hoof & Horn Club social event remembered fondly by all was the "nut fry", a dining experience which featured the testicles of castrated bulls. Better known by the gentry as "Mountain Oysters", or as "cojones" by the vaqueros, the pieces de resistance were abundant in the West Bottoms.

After an auction sale, the commission men, cattle buyers and shippers gathered at the Golden Ox. This could be the occasion for a party which, according to Jim Runyan, could get "pretty lively." Jim remembered that at one of them Mackey Woodley, a quiet but fun-loving Texan, suffered a very painful toothache and asked for help. Jim took him to a dentist who pulled the tooth. "Mackey said 'no anesthetic, I'm going back to the party' and he did."

COWTOWN

Cattle Trails And West Bottom Tales

The price dickering was among friends. Gene Furnish recalled this exchange between his father and Alfred Neuberger:

> "Ben was selling cattle and priced a load to Alfred. Alfred bid several times and Ben kept saying 'no'. Finally, Alfred said: 'I'm bidding you a good price on these cattle Ben. Why don't you sell them to me?' Ben said: 'I'm going to as soon as you quit bidding.'"

Carl Strobel was one of the most respected packer buyers in the stockyards. Ed Gorman was his trainee: assigned to run errands, check the alleys for the best cattle, and open gates. He also took care of Strobel's horse, Big Bert. When Big Bert was not in use, it was Gorman's responsibility to loosen his cinch strap so he would be more comfortable and able to eat and drink. It was even more important to tighten the cinch again for remounting. This process was critical in the case of Carl Strobel and his mount, a big man on a big horse. One sloppy day, his trainee failed to sufficiently tighten the cinch and the saddle slipped, propelling Strobel into the morass of mud and manure under the horse. Cliff Kaney was one of the amused spectators, and told Ed Gorman: "Boy, I think you'd better go check some yard pens." Ed did, in haste.

In his youth, Wayne Theis was a "jackpot" boy, a job reserved for rookies in the yards. "Jackpot" was the stockyards' name for small, varied lots of cattle. For several decades, cattle raised on small farms near Kansas City were collected by truckers in a mixed truckload (the jackpot) which might have several owners. It was the demanding job of the jackpot boy to take his jackpot to the scale for weighing, remembering the names of the respective owners. The job disappeared when the cattle population near Kansas City dwindled, and those that remained were sold at nearby small sale barns.

For many years, Don Huebner was the Hartford Insurance Company agent in the stockyards, selling insurance and performance bonds. He was transferred there from Louisville, Kentucky to handle the numerous claims following the 1951 flood — long after the 1917 fire losses, also covered by the Hartford. Don was an entrepreneur who saw opportunity in the absence of a hat check stand in the Golden Ox. The cattlemen prized their hats and he furnished a convenient place for their safekeeping during meals — for a price. Operated by an attractive young lady, his monopoly was a "gold mine" for several years. He claimed that it paid for his farm "before Dillingham took it away."

Norton Rixey provided a copy of "The History of the Kansas City Stockyards 1930 — 1980", a movie produced by Pete Stipetic and filmed by Gibbons Audio-Visual Productions of Olathe, Kansas. Stipetic was cattle buyer for Maurer-Neuer, and the movie is dedicated by him to William Maurer. It is authentic history which follows two cattle traders, buyer and seller, going about their dickering in the yards. They use their slender, rod-like whips to nudge cattle aside for closer examination and punctuate their negotiations with an emphatic nod of the head for "yes" or a less perceptible head shake for "no."

The movie opens with shots of traders watching as the day's prices are chalked on the Department of Agriculture's "scoreboard" in the Livestock Exchange Building and also devotes considerable

Cattle Trails And West Bottom Tales

footage to the 1951 flood, filming bedraggled cattle that had gone without feed or water for three days, debris forming a dam when plastered by the river's current against bridges, police boats, inoculations being administered to prevent infection, and a stranded hog patrolling the roof of a box car. Pete Stipetic comments that the yards were back in business after five weeks.

The cattlemen filmed over the years were all amiable and able-bodied, comfortable when sitting on a well-trained horse or perching on a fence or wading through the mud or dust of the alleys and pens, and constantly flicking their whips. Most wore western hats, and there was an occasional suit and tie worn by the likes of Jay Dillingham. The camaraderie was evident.

Scene in Stock Yards, with Kansas City on the horizon.
Noll postcard collection

COWTOWN

Cattle Trails And West Bottom Tales

CONCLUSION

The history of the West Bottoms and its occupants mirrors the ebb and flow of life in the heart of America. People gathered at the confluence of two large rivers in the middle of the country for many reasons. They came from all directions — North, South, East and West. Some passed through and some remained. And the Kansa were already here. There have been many chapters in their story to date.

Peter Fleck once declared: "History is the part of the past that has escaped oblivion, and in order to escape oblivion someone must testify." Come as You Are: Reflections of Everyday Life (1933), Beacon Press. If we lose a part of our past, we will be the poorer for it.

It is appropriate that the Jackson County Historical Society is one of this book's publishers, with its motto: "Dedicated to the future of the past." As Kansas City's leaders search for future development opportunities, they have rediscovered the past – the historic West Bottoms.

The new chapter will be recorded by future observers.

COWTOWN

Cattle Trails And West Bottom Tales

ACKNOWLEDGEMENTS AND BIBLIOGRAPHY

Steve Noll, Executive Director, Jackson County Historical Society, was not only a partner in this project but contributed pictures and source material from his own collections. The Society has been joined by the Mid-Continent Library in the publication of this book.

Sally Kaney Tourtellot Ruddy was another esteemed collaborator. It was she who suggested a book on the stockyards and provided the "Kaney's Kid" anecdotes and other stories and photos.

Robert Morris, artist and sculptor and source of "Stockyard Shaman" observations, urged broadening the scope of the narrative to include the entire West Bottoms, greatly enhancing this history and the pleasure of recording it.

The Husch Blackwell law firm provided support services in the production of the manuscript, with particular bows to legal administrative specialist Mary Stone and library assistant Susan Osborn.

The photography came largely from the Kansas City Star, thanks to Star Books publisher Doug Weaver, and from the special collections of the Missouri Valley Room, Kansas City Public Library, Kansas City, Missouri. Stockyard historian Alan Rogers provided not only images but accompanying narrative.

James Runyan Jr. of Swift & Henry rounded up old-timers for lunch-time reminiscences at the legendary Golden Ox Restaurant in the West Bottoms, and the American Royal's Cindy Stanley opened doors to the past.

Bernadette Soptick gave a tour of the Strawberry Hill Museum and a glimpse of the history of the Hill's settlers.

The Hon. Howard Sachs, Jean Dunn, Bev Platt and Dr. Anita Eagle supplied family lore otherwise unavailable.

Dr. Ralph Hall and Bill Kircher recalled a time when Everything Was Up to Date in Kansas City.

Most of the other individuals who made significant contributions of anecdotes and photographs are identified in the course of the book. They provided the human interest that is the heart of this history.

A bibliography of helpful publications includes Cowboys: The End if the Trail by Alton Pryor; Riders of the Chisholm Trail by James W. Parker; National Register of Historic Places, U. S. Department of the Interior, March 1992 by Sally E. Schwenk; Twenty Years of Kansas City's Live Stock and Traders by Cuthbert Powell; Kansas City Journal of Commerce, June 4, 1871; At the River's Bend , An Illustrated History of Kansas City by Sherry Lamb Schirmer and Richard D. McKenzie; Filthy Rich by Rick Montgomery, Kansas City Star, 1997; Life in a Pig Mill by A. L. Kovac Sr.; The Kansas City

COWTOWN

Cattle Trails And West Bottom Tales

Meat Packing Industry Before 1900, Missouri Historical Review, by G. K. Renner; Historical Sketches of Cattle Trails of the West and Southwest, by Joseph McCoy; The Cowboys, Time-Life Books 1973, Time Inc.; From the Bottom Up: The Story of the Irish in Kansas City by Pat O'Neill; Tom's Town: Kansas City and the Pendergast Legend by William N. Reding; Pendergast by Lawrence Larsen and Nancy Hulston; Kansas City: The Spirit, The People, The Promise, by Patricia Ewing Pace; The River Club, Its History and Development by Roger Swanson; Midwest Research Institute's Midcontinent Perspectives; Armour and Company (1867 – 1967), a Century of Public Service; The Grand Barbecue by Doug Worful; Charles Sumner Gleed Collection, Kansas State Historical Society; Kansas History, a Journal of the Central Plains; America's Historic Stockyards, Liestock Hotels, by J'Nell L. Pate; Kansas city Stockyards and Packing House Interests, 1899; Running out of Footprints by Cathy Callen; Kansas City Spirit by Bruce Mathews; Historic Kansas City's Possum Trot Gazette 1870 - 1890; The Kings and Queens of the Range by Mrs. John H. Gregory; Terminal Junction by Steven Dushan Milakov; Kansas City Illustrated Review, May 1, 1886; Images of Strawberry Hill by Marijana Grisnik; Overview of the East European Pan-Educational Institute by Sherry Lamb Schirmer; Flour Milling in America by Herman Steen; Rise and Fall of a Cowtown by Rick Montgomery; The Jungle by Upton Sinclair; The New Empire, June 1903; Charles P. Shipley Catalogue No. 9, c. 1911; The American Royal: 1899 – 1999, by Heather N. Paxton; It's All About Eating: Kansas City's History and Opportunity by John Dillingham; The Stockyard Shaman by Robert Morris; Leawood ; A Portrait in Time, by Ann Morris; The History of the Kansas City Livestock Market and the Kansas City Stockyards Company 1871 – 1985 by Jay Dillingham; Kansas City Illustrated Review May 1, 1886; Time Magazine July 14, 1947; Armour Family History by Edwin Shutt; Saddle and Sirloin Club History by Bill and Sue Symon; BOTAR Fiftieth Anniversary Book, 1949 - 1999; Kansas City Design Center/Urban Design Studio, 2010 Analysis; Dut to Destiny – It's Just the Cowboy in Me by Walt Krier; Texas Monthly Magazine, February 1974; A Short History of Possum Trot, 1974 – 1986, by David W. Jackson; The History of Barbecue 101, Fiorella's Jack Stack Barbecue; Kansas City business Magazine, May 2003; and Kansas City Veterinary College 1891 – 1918, The Foundation of the Kansas City Animal Health Corridor by Howard H. Erickson; Blueprint for Disaster, by Disaster Corps Inc., 1951.

A movie produced by Pete Stipec confirmed stockyards' lore about the informal ways of traders; The History of the Kansas City Stockyards 1930 – 1980 was filmed by Gibbons Audio – Visual Productions of Olathe, Kansas.

COWTOWN

Cattle Trails And West Bottom Tales

ILLUSTRATIONS

Pictures from Missouri Valley Room Special Collection, Kansas City Public Library, Kansas City, Missouri are identified as Missouri Valley Room photos.

Pictures from Twenty Years of Kansas City's Live Stock and Traders are identified as Twenty Years photos.

Pictures from Mrs. S. J. Ray's postcard collection, Missouri Valley Room are identified as Ray postcard collection, and Steve Noll photographs and postcards are identified as such.

COWTOWN

Cattle Trails And West Bottom Tales

ABOUT THE AUTHOR

EDWARD T. MATHENY, JR., was a history major at the University of Missouri, where he played varsity basketball and was elected to Phi Beta Kappa. A Navy veteran of World War II, he served on the staff of Fleet Admiral Chester Nimitz and also participated in the occupation of Japan. A *cum laude* graduate of Harvard Law School, he practiced law for more than 50 years.

He was a founder and first president of KCPT (Kansas City's public television station), Chancellor of the Episcopal Diocese of West Missouri, president of Saint Luke's Hospital, a chairman of the Eye Foundation, and served on various corporate and non-profit boards. The Edward T. Matheny Jr. Missouri Endowed Chair of Neuroscience was established in 1998 at St. Luke's Marion Bloch Neuroscience Institute. He is a member of the Missouri Academy of Squires and this is his seventh history book on a subject of local interest.

INDEX

Note: An asterisk (*) indicates a photo or other illustration.

A

A. J. Kelly Iron Foundry, 22
Abernathy Brothers, furniture factory, 29
Abernathy Warehouse Building, destruction by fire, 66
Abilene, Kansas
    Chisholm Trail ended in, 4
    cowboys found recreation in, 17
    founding of, 17
    shipping yard, 5
Adams, Charles Francis, 27
Adams family, 62
"The Adventure of a Mule," 55
AFA (Agriculture Future of America), 144
Agricultural Business Council of Kansas City, 93
Alexander vs. Crotchett et al, 53
American cowboy, characteristics of, 5
American Hereford Association building, 125, 125*
American Hereford Cattle Breeders' Association, 69
American House hotel, 22
American Royal, 68–71
    advertisement (1940), 114*
    arena, 69, 71*
    Bar B-Q contest, 142
    economic impact on the Kansas City area, 146
    Mrs. Combs star of, 133
    1902 version, 68*
    permanent and adequate home for, 69
    supporters of, 111–114
    visits to, 132
American Royal Building
    in 1928, 70*
    construction in 1921, 69
    deteriorated over the years, 138
    falling apart by 1987, 150
American Royal Centennial, in 1999, 139
American Royal complex, 69
American Royal Parade, first in 1926, 70
American Royal Show (1905), 69*
American Shorthorn Cattle Breeders' Association, 69
American Steel and Wire Plant, destruction by fire, 66
Amigoni Urban Winery, 36, 150
animal health industry, mid-America's burgeoning, 146
Annunciation Parish, establishment of, 20
Annunciation Parish hall, 20*
Apaches, 80
Arabia riverboat, 5
Arabia Steamboat Museum, 5
Arabian Horse Show, 146
Armour(s), 2, 15
Armour, Andrew Watson, 42
Armour, Annie, 145
Armour, Kirkland, 145
Armour, Phillip Danforth, 14
Armour, Simeon Brooks, 14, 38, 42
Armour & Company, 14, 56
Armour Brothers Banking Company, 105
Armour farm home at 6740 Pennsylvania, 145
Armour Meatpacking Company, 14, 27, 110, 118
    animal dis-assembly line, 28, 28*
    expansion, 46, 46*
    plant near the Missouri – Kaw River junction, 16*
    plant steam whistle, 15
Armour name, everywhere in Kansas City, 145
Army engineers, favored construction of the Tuttle Creek Dam, 119
arsenic, led to the eradication of Texas fever, 77
Aslin, Malcolm (Mick), 150
Attebury, Duke, 98
Auburn High School, in Kansas, 132
auction chant, ideal, 136
auction crowd, group picture of, 135*
auction sales, preferable to trading "on the bricks," 134
auctioneers, 136
Autry, Gene, 58
    steers owned by, 58*

B

Baldy quarter horse, 145
Baltimore Hotel, 70
Bank of Kansas City, 38
banking services, as pioneer stockyards enterprises, 37
barbecue capital, Kansas City becoming, 143
barbed wire, invention ended the open range, 19

INDEX

barbers, in the West Bottoms, 13
bare-knuckle fights, staged in stockyard pens,
  54
Barnum & Bailey, 133
Barr, Bill, 99
Barr, Herbert J., 99
Barr, Jack, 99, 99*
Barr, Ken, 99, 99*
Bartle, H. Roe, 149
Bartling, Howard G., 63
Bass,Tom, 75
Bassett, Charlie, 22
Battenfeld Grease, 120
Belles of the American Royal (BOTAR), 112
Benson, Ezra Taft, 125, 126, 126*
Benton, Thomas Hart, 26, 123
Berkley, Richard, 141, 144
Big Alice, 128
Big Bert (horse), 156
Bigger, Thomas, 27
Bill Haw Cowboy sculpture, 153*
biosciences industry, Kansas City area, 148
blizzard of 1886, killed hundreds of head, 146
blood donors, for Cliff Kaney, 91
Blossom, George Newton, 30, 35, 41
Blossom House hotel, 35, 35*, 41, 64
"Bob Potee's Number Three Faro Bank"
  gambling hall, 22
Bolte, Carl, 113, 120–121
Bon Ami, Faultless acquired by, 154
boot scrape and a water trough with brushes,
  outside the Livestock Exchange Building, 115,
  130
BOTAR Ball (1963), in Municipal Auditorium,
  113*
BOTAR Fiftieth Anniversary Book, 1949-1999,
  112
Bowery, Union Avenue society compared to, 23
Bozich, Kata, 48
Branton, Mary Shaw (Shawsie), 131
Branton, W. Coleman, 110
Bread King, 73
brick packing houses, collapsed in 1903 flood,
  55
Bricker, Bob, 155
bridal couples, lodge banners accompanied, 52
bridges, lost in the West Bottoms, 55
brisket, identifying the steer with the best, 130
British Boer War, 148
"The Bronco Buster," at Kansas City's Nelson –
  Atkins Museum of Art, 19

Brooks, Alvin, 141
Bryant Building, 55
buffalo bones, 8, 8*
buffalo herds, commercial slaughter of, 8
buffalo hide, converted into commercial leather,
  8
Bull Mountain land art, 151, 151*
bulls
  ordinary dangerous, 53
  testicles of castrated, 155
Bureau of Animal Industry (B.A.I.), 148
Burnett, Florence, 46, 55
Burnett, William E., 46, 55
Burnett Meat Co., 55
Burns, Bob, 98
business progress, 29–30
butcher trade, effect of ruthless labor practices,
  147
Butler, William. See Hickok, Wild Bill
Butz, Earl, 139
buyer and seller negotiating the price, 92*

C
cable car, 40*, 40–41
cable incline, Ninth Street, 41*
Campbell Taggart Associated Bakeries, 74
"Canada Bill," 22
Carrillo, Leo, 113
cartoon, "Still the Greatest Cow Town in
  America," 103, 103*
Case Park, 23
Cassidy Southeastern Commission Co., 129
cattle
  auction, last on September 26, 1991, 144
  driven by men on horseback to the packing
    plants, 14
  drives, instituted after the Civil War, 4
  evolution from gaunt, durable Texas
    Longhorns to purebreds, 68
  on trail from Texas, 9*
  trails from Texas to northern railheads, 4
cattle long horns, collection of antique, 129
"Cattle Marketing in the American Southwest:
  The Rise of the Kansas City Commission
  Merchant in the Nineteenth Century," 6
cattlemen
  looking for a good time in Kansas City, 18
  riding horses to work, 75
"Central Industrial District," name adopted for
  the West Bottoms in 1923, 119
Central Packing Company, 95

Champ Clark (grand champion mule), 98
Charbonneau, Jean-Baptiste, 25
Charles P. Shipley Saddlery and Mercantile
  Company, 58, 60*, 116, 127
Cherokee, 116
chewing tobacco, favored over cigars and
  cigarettes, 115
Chicago, linkage of Kansas City to, 6
Chicago World's Fair: Columbian Exposition,
  39
Chisholm, Jesse, 4, 58
Chisholm Trail, 4, 77
City Council of Kansas City, Missouri, 7
City of Kansas, settlement of, 2
City of Leawood, Kansas, 80, 81*
Civil War, obstructed cattle movements, 4
Clark, Champ, 98
Clark, William, 25, 119–120
Climax race horse, 22
Coates House, 27
Cochran, Wendell, 140
Cody, Buffalo Bill, 17, 19*
coin flip, resolving differences, 91
"cojones," 155
Colorado Eagle, 101
Columbian Steel Tank Company, 39, 39*, 104,
  120, 120*
Combs, Loula Long, 133*, 133–134
Commerce Bancshares, 105
Commerce Bank, 122
Commerce Trust Company, 122, 127
commercial bakeries, establishment of, 73–74
commercial district, opening into the Bottoms, 7
commercial exchange, maintaining, 33
commission firms, employed solicitors, 32
commission houses, 34
Commonwealth Aircraft Company, occupied
  the American Royal building during WW II,
  103
Convention Hall, 46, 46*
conveyor line, 27
Cook, Linda, 141
Corps of Discovery Monument, 25, 25*
Corps of Discovery of Lewis & Clark, 2, 25
Cortes, Hernando, 4
Coulson, Janelle, 114*
county banks, passed in and out of existence, 37
cowboy on horseback, bronze sculpture of, 152
cowboys, 17–19
  payday capers of, 17
  Remington's representation as heroic, 18

The Cowboys (photo), 19*
"cowpoke," 100
"Cow-Town Coffee Shop," 115
cowtown past, also part of Kansas City's future,
  138
crap game, in a cattle chute, 107
Crazy Alice, 29
Croation businesses, patronized by Croation
  workers, 50
Cudahy Packing Co., 118, 122, 129

D
"Daily Drovers Telegram," 36, 37
Daily Live Stock Record, 36
Dalton, William J., 20
dance hall, 18*
Darby, Harry, 112, 120, 126–127, 149
Darby Products of Steel Company,
  manufactured landing craft during WW II, 103
Daub, Eugene L., 25, 25*
Davis, Ray, 144
Dead Hog Detail, 122
"Dead Man's Curve" at Grand Avenue, 40
Deere, John, 29
Deere, Mansur & Co., 29
Depression years, out of work men, 86
Deramus, William, II, 87
Dewar and Smith, 44
Diamond Mills, 44
DiCapo, Carl, 148
The Dillingham(s), 93–97
Dillingham, Jay B., 1, 93, 93*, 94, 95, 95*, 104,
  126–127, 135*, 157
Dillingham, John, 69, 95*, 95–96, 97, 126, 127,
  148
Dillingham, W. J. (Joe), 94, 94*
Dillingham and Hudson, 94
Dillingham Enterprises, 96
Dillingham Freeway Bridge, 94, 120
Dillon, Joan, 102, 141
"Disaster Corps, Inc.," 122
Doggett, Frederick S., 63*
Dole, Robert, 149, 149*
drawing straws, for first pick, 90, 90*
"drovers," cowboys as, 19
Drovers hotel, 38
Drovers Telegram building, 150
Dubois, J. H., 8
"Dubois hide house," 8
Duncan, David Douglas, 113
Dunn, Jean Aylward, 46, 55

INDEX

E
Eagle, Agnes, 51
Eagle, Alexander (Alec) Renwick, 27, 51, 147
Eagle, John (Jack), 27, 147
Eagle, Richard, 148
Eagle, Robert, 27, 147
Eagle, Thomas J., 27, 148
Eagle, Thomas McCauley, 148
Eagle, William, 147
Eagle Animal Hospital, in Riverside, Missouri, 148
Eagle Anti-Cholera Serum, 148
Eagle Biological and Supply Co., 148
Eagle Laboratories, 148
earthy humor, prevailed in pens and alleys of the stockyards, 155
Edith and Harry Darby Foundation, 150
Edwards, Roy A., Jr., 112
Eighth Street tunnel, leading to Quality Hill, 42
8th Street Tunnel, entrance to, 43*
Eisenhower, Dwight D., 125, 126, 127, 149
Ellsworth, Kansas, replaced Abilene as the Chisholm Trail hot-spot, 18
Elmwood Cemetery, Armours interred in, 145
Englewood, Kansas, 131
Enid and Crosby Kemper Foundation, 68
epitaphs, of cowboys, 17
Evans, Ray, 112
Evans – Snider – Buell Co., 83
exchange building. *See also* Livestock
  Exchange Building
    at 12th Street and State Line, 10
    drawing of first 1871, 10*
    new completed in 1886, 31
Exchange Hall, 62*, 97, 129
exchange shelter, improvement to, 13, 13*
exchanges, conducting in a structure keeping out the rain and cold, 10
Exodus Family (sculpture), 143

F
"fainting couch," 96
Fairbanks scales, 10, 13, 118
Famous Stock Yards Saddle, 59
fan dancer, performance, 102
farm implement distribution center, Kansas City as, 29
fat stock show, purpose of, 68
Faultless 8th Street Campus Project, 154
Faultless Starch/ Bon Ami, 154

Faultless Starch company brochure, 153
Faultless Starch Library books, 153–154
Faultless West Bottoms plant, 154
Faultless/Bon Ami world headquarters office building, 154, 154*
Ferdinand the Bull, saga of, 53
FFA (Future Farmers of America), 70, 144
fights, staged, 54*
fire (1917), 65
fire proof vaults, in the new Livestock Exchange Building, 63
fires, 65–67
First National Bank, 80, 122
Flaherty, Mark, 131–132, 132*, 144
Fleck, Peter, 158
flood(s), constant menace to stockyards, 55–57
flood (1903), 55–56, 56*, 57*
flood (1908), 56, 57*
flood (1951), 1, 117–124
  destruction everywhere, 124*
  marooned animals, 124*
  photo, 118*
flood control, 119
"Flood Disaster" (lithograph), 123
flour mills, 44
Fogel, Jerry, 104
Folger, Evans, 121
Folly Theatre, 101, 102
  building, 102*
  headliner, 102*
Food and Drug Act, 110
4-H Clubs (Head, Heart, Hands, Health), 70
Fowler Brothers Packing House, 14
  employees, 15*
Franco, Francisco, 108
"Fred Owen Mules," 104
Fred Platt Horse Barn, 82
Freedom Trail, 143
Frevert, Anita Eagle, 27, 147
Frisco line, 39
"From the Bottom Up: The Story of the Irish in Kansas City," 20
"Frontier Kansas City" (mural), 26
Furnish, Ben, 155, 156
Furnish, Gene, 155, 156
Future Farmers of America (the FFA), 70, 144

G
Gaitan, Fernando, Jr., 14
Gaitan, Fernando, Sr., 14
Gaitan, Jose, 14

Galloway cattle, importing and breeding, 81
gamblers, 22
Genesee Royale Bistro, 150
Genessee Bar, 137
Genessee Inn, 140
Genessee Street
    drinking and dancing, 128
    spelling of, 116
George IV Phaeton roadster, 133
Gillespie, A. J., 33
Gillham, Robert, 40
Gillham Road, 40
Gilmore, Tommy, 130
Glass, Clara, 23
Glass, Moritz, 23
Glass family, 23
Glass Labyrinth, 77, 78*
Gleed, Charles, 29
gliders, production of, 103
Golden Ox Restaurant, 1, 1*, 113, 115, 132, 142
    absence of a hat check stand in, 156
    cowboy photo, 97*
    general manager of, 144
    lunch-time gatherings at, 155–157
    parties at, 155
Good, Ferdinand (Ferd), 104, 108, 155
Gorman, Ed, 155, 156
grain, shipped to the West Bottoms for storage, 44
grain elevators, in the West Bottoms, 44
Great Western Paint Company, 121
Gregory, Mrs. John H., 42
Grimes, Robert, 147
gripman, 40
Grisnik, Marijana, 49
grist mill, Splitlog built, 51
Groucho Marx program, on television, 147
Gulf of Mexico, linking Kansas City to, 38
Gustin Bacon Manufacturing Co., 120
Guyton & Harrington mule firm, 29, 98

H
Hadley, William M., 83
Haggard's Locker Room, Billiard parlor and Shoe Shine parlor, 137
Hale, Joe and Joyce, 150
Hall, Joyce C., 122
Hall, Muggins, 136
Hall, Ralph, 99*, 99–101
Hall Family Foundation, 150
Hammerstein, Oscar, 101

Hannibal & St. Joseph, railroad station on Union Avenue in 1890, 8
Hannibal Bridge, 6–7, 7*
Harrison, President, 35
Hartford Fire Insurance Company
    covered much of 1917 fire loss, 65
    panoramic photo of 1917 fire, 66*
    photo of 1917 fire, 67*
Hartford Insurance Company agent, 156
Hastings, G. Richard, 128
hats, sold by Shipley, 59
Haun, Amy, 112
Haw, William, 150, 151
Haw Ranches office
    headquartered in the Livestock Exchange Building, 150
    saddle residing in, 152
Hawley, Greg, 5
Hazlett, O. James, 6, 31
"Hell's Half Acre" neighborhood, 20
"help yourself" sign, 86
Henry, Charles D., 83
Herb Schreiner program, on television, 147
Hereford bull, looking down on the West Bottoms, 125, 125*
Hibbard, Fredrick C., 24
Hickok, Wild Bill, 17–18, 19*, 22
Historic Hyde Park District, 82
"The History of Kansas City Stockyards 1930-1980" (movie), 156
The History of the Kansas City Livestock Market And The Kansas City Stock Yards Company 1871-1985, 94
Hockaday, Laura, 113
hog butcher knife, used by Thomas J. Eagle at Armour & Co., 27*
Hogan, Edward "Muskogee," 143
Holy Family Church, 50
Honeywood estate, 12
Hoof and Horn Club, 96
    Christmas Parties at, 155
    rooms of, 62
hoof and mouth disease, eliminating in cattle, 148
horn furniture, largest piece of, 129*
Horner, Bill, 107, 107*, 119
horse and mule markets, to the British government for WW I, 65
horse cars, 40
horsemen, paraded down Genesee Street, 75
Horvat, Anton, 110

Hotel Muehlbach, reception for Trujillo, 127, 127*
hotels, in the West Bottoms, 38
Hovey, Robert (Bob) D., 114*, 142
Huebner, Don, 155, 156
"Hump" (Himalayan Mountains), 148
Hunter, John B., 12
Hunter, Lem, 12
Hyde Park District land, 82

I
I. A. O'Shaughnessy/Wysong Family Foundations, 150
"I'm From Missouri" (movie), 98, 98*
insurance, immigrants unable to afford, 52
Intercity Viaduct, construction of, 56
Interstate National Bank, 38, 122
the Irish, 20–21
Irish families, forced out of the Bottoms, 55
Iroquois, 116

J
"jackpot" boy, 156
Jackson Country Historical Society, 158
"Jackson County Insane Asylum," 30
Jay B. Dillingham Award for Agricultural Leadership & Excellence, 93
J.C. Penny, 113
Jennings, Waylon, 19
Jessee, Randall, 96
John B. Stetson hats, 59
Journal of Commerce, editor and owner of, 11
"The Jungle," 53, 110

K
Kaney, Clifton John (Cliff), 83, 84, 85, 85*, 86, 128, 156
    collapse with a bleeding ulcer, 91
    election as president of the Kansas City, Missouri Chamber of Commerce, 94
    on a Monday morning at the stockyards, 88*
"Kaney's Kid," 83
Kansa Indians, 2, 141
Kansas City
    beginnings of, 2
    first railroad station, 8*
    terminal of the Shawnee Trail, 4
Kansas City Area Life Sciences Institute, 148
Kansas City Board of Trade, organized in 1869, 44
Kansas City Fat Stock Show Association, 68, 82

Kansas City Flood edition, June, 1903, 55
Kansas City Horse & Mule Commission Co., 108*
Kansas City Livestock Exchange. See Livestock Exchange
Kansas City Missouri Junior League, 141
Kansas City Museum, 133
Kansas City Southern Belle steam-engine, bell from, 87, 87*
Kansas City Southern Railway Company, 38
Kansas City Stock Yards, 45*
    closed, 144–145
    livery barn, 61*
    ownership transferred, 144
    pen, commission men in, 34*
    rebuilding program, 63
Kansas City Stock Yards Bank, 38
Kansas City Stock Yards Company, 27, 62, 69, 93
Kansas City Stockyards Company, 138, 144
Kansas City Suburban Belt Railway, 38
Kansas City Terminal Railway, 64
Kansas City Union Stock Yards, image of Texas cattle in, 11*
Kansas City Veterinary College, 146*, 146–147
Kansas Pacific Railway, 6, 33
Kansas State University, veterinary medicine school, 146
Kansas Stockyards, 12
    photograph of in 1873, 12*
Kansas Stockyards Company, 14, 15, 27
Kauffman, Muriel, 141
Kaw River
    1903 flood, 56
    1951 flood, 117
Kaw River frontage, 150
Kaw River water, "very disagreeable taste," 51
Kemper, Alexander (Sandy), 144
Kemper, James and Jonathan, 150
Kemper, James M., Jr., 105, 105*
Kemper, Jonathan, 25, 150
Kemper, Mariner, 150
Kemper, R. Crosby, Jr., 138–139, 139*, 144, 150
Kemper, R. (Rufus) Crosby, Sr., 138
Kemper, William Thornton, 105, 138, 150
Kemper Arena
    birth of, 138
    future prospects, 150
    photo, 138*
    roof collapsed in 1979, 142

Kenwood Golf Links, 82
Kerr, Day, 141
Kinnear, W. J., 64*
Kircher, William, 102
Kirk, Charlotte Wornall, 130
knife fights, on pay day, 53
"knocking" pen, 155
Kramer, Andrew, 39
Krier, Walt, 131

L
labor problems, contributed to relocation of
  West Bottom meat packers, 110
lard, refining of, 14
Lathrop, Missouri, 29
lead cow, 155
Leaf, Munro, 53
Leathers,Tom, 141
Leavenworth penitentiary, cattle bought by, 130
Leawood, Kansas, 80, 81*
Lee's Summit, Missouri, old Kaney farm in, 87
Lentz, Dickie, 122
Lentz, Mr. and Mrs. D.S., 122
Leoti, Kansas, 101
Levi, Dollie, 92
Lewis, Meriwether, 25
Lewis & Clark, 2
Lewis and Clark Point, 23, 25, 26
Lewis and Clark Trail Heritage Foundation, 25
Lewis and Clark Viaduct, 56
Live Stock Exchange Building, entrance to
  (1887), 31*
"Live Stock" trade, 33
livestock
  establishing the sale price of a load of, 131
  shipped to smaller, modern packing plants,
    144
livestock commission merchants, 31–34
livestock commission system, 32
Livestock Exchange
  with bylaws, 33
  improved moral tone of the livestock
    industry, 33
  isolating Texas Longhorns, 77
Livestock Exchange Building, 116. See also
  exchange building
  additions to, 46–47
  banking rooms in, 37
  border between two states running through,
    47, 47*
  born in the same year as Jay Dillingham, 94

damaged by water in 1903 flood, 55
  general manager of, 144
  illustration of, 38*
  larger opened in 1911, 62
  owner of, 150
  "scoreboard" in, 156
  second in 1876, 29
  survives, 145
livestock judging contests, Royal's, 70
livestock market, Kansas City a complete by the
  mid-1870s, 29
Livestock National Bank, 152
livestock publications, 36
livestock trade, "a man's word was his bond,"
  82
livestock trucks, unloading at Kansas City
  Stockyards, 76*
locomotives, replaced riverboats, 6
lodges, 52
Long, Mrs. R. A., 133
Long, Robert A., 133
Long Horn hat, 59
longhorn bulls, with long, sharp horns, 4
longhorn steers
  broken for draft duty, 40
  Gene Autry's awaiting the packing house
    hammer, 58*
long-horned cattle, of Spain, 4
Longview Farm, in Lee's Summit, Missouri,
  133
Loose, Jacob, 74
Loose, John L., 74
Loose Park, 82
Loose-Wiles Biscuit Company, 74*
Loula Long carriage, at the American Royal
  Museum, 134*
Loveless family quartette (Harmon, Merman,
  Lela, and Lola), 147, 147*

M
Mackey, Edmonds P. (Bud), 144
Mackey, G. Edmonds, 110
Madison, Guy, 111
"Mammas Don't Let Your Babies Grow Up To
  Be Cowboys," 19
Manor Baking Company, 74
marketing news service, provided by United
  States Department of Agriculture, 115
Marshall, Bill, 76
Massman, John, 122
Mastin Bank, 80

Mathews, Bruce, 38, 55, 94
Maurer, William, 156
Maurer-Neuer Inc., 110
McCoy, Joseph Geiting (Joe), 4, 5, 5*, 17,
    32–33
McCrosky, Thomas G., 63*
McGonigle, Bill, 55
McGonigle's market, 55
McKie,Paul, 134
Meat Inspection Act, 110
meat packers, first introduced the concept of the
    conveyor line, 27
meat packing, as Kansas City's major industry
    by 1896, 46
meat packing plants, attracted unskilled
    peasants, 48
meatpacking center, Kansas City slow but
    steady decline as, during the 1950s and 60s,
    118
memories, of the stockyards, 128–132
Mennonites, from Southern Russia, 44
Metropolitan Hotel, 68
Metropolitan Street Railway Company, 42
Metzger, Syl, 130
Midwest Research Institute, 148
Milakov, Steven Dushan, 43, 152
Miller, John E., 112
milling business, successful, 44
Miss Rex waltzing mare, 75
Missouri Pacific Railroad, 6, 101
Missouri River
    settlement on, 2
    steamboat at the foot of Main Street in 1880,
    6*
Mix, Tom, 58
Moffitt, John C., 98
Mohawk Indian, 51
Mohler, John R., 148
Montgomery, Rick, 145
Morehead, Hugh, 136, 144
Morris, Edward, 63
Morris, Robert, 77, 78*, 89, 91, 120, 151
Morris Packing Firm, 83
Morse, Charles F., 27
Morse, George, 136
Morse, L. V., 10, 13
motorized wrangler, plight of, 140, 140*
"Mountain Oysters," 155
movie, about the stockyards, 156–157
mule cars, 40, 43*
mules, 98

adopted as state animal, 29
market for, 29, 65
Mexican market for, 108
in World War I, 1
in World War II, 148

N
Nadeau, Virginia Jennings, 112–113
Nast, William F., 115
National Agricultural Center And Hall of Fame
    move to the West Bottoms, 148–149
    photos, 149*
National Bank of Commerce, branch of, 38
National Championship Saddlebred Horse
    Competition, 146
National Hereford Show, 68
National Texas Longhorn Museum, 129
Neff, Jay Holcomb, 37, 37*
Neff Hall, University of Missouri's, 37
Nelson – Atkins Museum of Art, 19
Nesbat, John, 153
Neuberger, Alfred, 155, 156
New Empire, 55
Nichols, J.C., 1
Ninth Street cable line, elevated terminal in the
    West Bottoms, 42*
"nut fry," Hoof & Horn Club social event, 155
Nutter, James A., 33–34
Nutter, James B., 33
Nutter, Natis M., 33
Nutter Bros., 33

O
O'Boynick, Paul, 50
O'Brien, Joey, 109*
"Oklahoma," 101
Olander, Fred, 104, 107, 119, 126, 126*, 134,
    135*
Olander, Fred, Jr., 104
Olander, Jonathan Wilhelm, 104
Oldham, Loy (Slick), 99, 101
Omohundro, Texas Jack, 17
O'Neill, Pat, 20, 22
Orin Haggard's Locker Room, change of clothes
    in lockers in, 107
Owen, Ferdinand (Ferd) Lincoln, 104, 108–109
oxen, counted among legitimate holdings of a
    sales stable, 40
Oxydol soap powder, 14

P

packers, 14–16

Packers & Stockyards Act, 33

packing houses
    discards, making use of, 14
    floors, blood on, 53
    labor unrest and union disputes, 110
    living conditions of workers, 48
    operations diminished after the 1951 flood, 118
    production, 103

packing plants, small with limited capacity at first, 14

Palmolive Peet Soap Company, 14

Parker, James W., 5

passenger train activity, by railroads, 39

Patch (neighborhood), 48, 49

"The Patch" (painting), 49*

Pawnee, Oklahoma, 86

Pawnee Bill, 86

Paxton, Heather N., 68, 133, 142, 150

Peet Brothers Soap Works, 14

Pendergast, James (Jim), 22–23, 55
    statue of, 23–24, 24*

Pendergast, Tom, 23, 24, 54

Penn Valley Park, 2*

pig lifting, 102

Pinter, Rudy, 155

Pioneer Mother Memorial, 2*

Pipkin, C. M., 17

Plankington & Armour packing plant, 14

The Platt(s), 80–82

Platt, Beverly, 82

Platt, Fred, 82

Platt, Mortimer R., 80*, 80–82

Platt, Roy, 82

politics, rougher side of, 54

Possum Trot, 2, 141

Possum Trot Award (1979), 142

Possum Trot festival
    1977 Gazette group picture of participants, 141, 142*
    brought to the West Bottoms, 141

Possum Trot Gazette, 40
    historic picture of Union Avenue, 141, 141*

Potee, Bob, 22

Powell, Cuthbert, 32, 33, 36, 36*, 94

Pressley, Laurence, 114*

Price Current, livestock paper, 36

printing plant, catered to the local packing houses, 38

Proctor & Gamble (P & G), 14–15

professional gamblers, 22

Pryor, Alton, 4, 19

public auction building, in 1969, 134

Putsch, Jud, 113

Putsch's 210 Restaurant, 113

Q

Quality Hill, near Lewis and Clark Point, 27

quarantine facilities, need for, 77

Quinn, Tommy, 120

R

R. Crosby Kemper Sr. Memorial Arena, 139

"Racehorse" McMorrow, 140

rail hub, Kansas City as by 1877, 29

railroad tracks, down the middle of First Street, 50

railroads, 40

Rand, Sally, 102

Ray, S. J., 103

Reardon, Jack, 144

recreation, taking its toll, 54

Red Martin, cowboy, 97*

Reddig, William, 64

Redhefer, Fred N., 121

Remington, Frederic, 18–19

Republican National Convention, in Kemper Arena in July 1976, 139

Research and Budget Department, of Kansas City, Missouri, 117

Resovich, Kata Bozich, 52*

Resovich, Mile, 48

Richard Robbins Anchor D Ranch, 134

River Club, 26, 26*, 121

riverboats, brought passengers and freight to Kansas City, 5

Riverfront Heritage Trail, 143, 150

Rixey, Norton, 155, 156

Robert Morris Bull Wall, 151*

Roberts, Joe, 127

Roberts, Roy, 149

Rockwell, Norman, 122

Rogers, Alan, 11, 12, 31, 129

Rogers, Richard, 101

Rogers, Roy, 58

Rogers, Will, 58, 70

Roosevelt, Franklin, 58

Roosevelt, Theodore, 35

Royal Rupert Hereford bull, 113

Royal Show, in England, 68

INDEX

Ruddy, Sally Kaney Tourtellot, 83, 85, 85*, 86, 87, 89, 91, 112, 113, 127, 134
Ruff, Emil, 73
Runyan, James L., Jr., 79*, 84, 105
Runyan, James, Sr., sorting cattle, 75*
Runyan, Jim, 79, 122, 128, 155
Runyan, Jim, 85
Russell, Janet Redhefer, 121
Russell, William, 121, 121*
Russian Orthodox Church, 50, 50*

S
Sacagawea, 25
Sachs, Howard F., 23
Saddle & Sirloin Club, 111
    Santa Fe, 1947, 111*
Saddle & Sirloin Wall of Fame, 136
The Saga of the Armour Family in Kansas City, 14
sale platform, level with the ground, 13
saloonkeepers, in the Irish community as politicians, 22
Sambol Meat Packing Company, 155
Sanders, George, 130
Santa Fe Railroad, 111
    filling its own grain elevators, 44
    grain elevators, in 1939, 44*
Satchell, Michael J., 144
Saxony black stallion, 127
scales. *See* Fairbanks scales
Scalpers, 32
Schauffler, Eduard R., 55
scholarly gamblers, 22
Seaman, Lewis's dog, 25
Senecas, 116
Shawnee Indian Mission, Fairway, KS, 4*
Shawnee Indian Mission buildings, in Fairway Kansas, 4
Shawnee Trail, 4
sheep market, "reopening," 122
Shipley, Charles, 58
Shipley building, 137, 137*
Shipley Saddlery. *See* Charles P. Shipley Saddlery and Mercantile Company
Shipley saddles, demand for, 58–59
Shutt, Edwin, 110, 118
"the Silicon Valley," of agriculture, 148
Silver King saddle, 59, 59*
Sims, Ray, 136
Sinclair, Upton, 53, 110
"slaughtermen," 27

slave exodus, depicting in sculpture, 143
Slavic population, moving up from the Bottoms onto the Hill, 50
Slovenian lodge, 52
"smart Alec" youngster, 128
Smith, Jerome, 11
Smith, Jerry, 141
"soap operas," 15
social front, in the 1870s, 29
Soden, Mary, 112
solicitors, 32
Soptick, Bernadette, 48, 50, 52
Sosland(s), 45
Sosland, Abe, 45
Sosland, Benjamin, 45
Sosland, David, 45, 72, 72*
Sosland, Fannie Mae, 45
Sosland, Henry, 45, 56
Sosland, Hymie, 45
Sosland, Louis, 45
Sosland, Morris, 45
Sosland, Morton, 92
Sosland, Samuel (Sam), 45, 56, 72, 72*
Sosland, Sanders, 45, 72, 72*
Sosland Publishing Company, beginning of, 72
Southwest Boulevard, city's largest Irish neighborhood, 21
Southwest High School, 113
Southwestern Miller (1944), 72–73, 73*, 105*, 106*
Spencer, Tom, 128
Spigarelli, Jim, 148
"The Spirit of Kansas City" (painting), 122, 123*
spittoons, 96, 115
Splitlog, Mathias, 38, 51
Splitlog Line (railroad), 38
Sprint Center, construction of, 150
spurs, manufacture of, 58
Squanto, 149, 149*
St. Anthony's Church, 50
St. John's Catholic Church, 50
St. Louis hotel, 38
St. Mary's Church, 50
St. Patrick's Day Parade
    earliest known photo, 21*
    Kansas City's first 1873, 20
state line, exchange building straddled in the 1800s, 47
State Line House, 6
steel tanks, 104

Steen, Herman, 72

steer horns, mounted sets of, 129

Stenerud, Jan, 141

Stern Brothers, 138

"Still the Greatest Cow Town in America"
   (cartoon), 103, 103*

Stilwell, Arthur E., 38

Stipetic, Pete, 156, 157

stock watering tanks and grain bins, 39

Stock Yards Bank, 38

"stock yards" builder, 33

Stock Yards National Bank, 38, 105, 138

stockyard business practices, built upon an
   atmosphere of trust, 90

stockyard cattle traders, retired, swapping
   stories, 155

stockyard employees, lawsuits by, 53

Stockyard Harness Company, 58

stockyard rangers, on horseback during World
   War II, 104

stockyards, 10–13
   1917 fire, 65
   activity, 75–79
   arranging docks for truckers to unload in
      Kansas or Missouri, 76
   banks in, 37
   camaraderie in a locker room environment,
      91
   dangerous work, 53
   entrance of the old, 152
   legacies of, 146–149
   memories of, 128–132
   sale and closure of, 144
   scene in, 157*
   unskilled workers, 48
   visitors of note, 125–127

Stockyards Company, required by federal
   statute to furnish facilities to any and all
   shippers, 53

Stockyards District, art at the entrance to, 152*

Stockyards Hotel, 38, 128, 136

Stockyards National Bank, 122

Strawberry Hill
   community of Catholic and ethnic people, 50
   extension of the West Bottoms, 48–52
   Mathias Splitlog built a house, 51, 51*

Strawberry Hill Museum and Cultural Center,
   48, 51

streetcar system, Kansas City best by January
   1,1897, 42

Strobel, Carl, 92, 156

Studna, Morris, 91

Sturdevant, Dan C.D., 25

Sunshine Biscuit factory, fire in the abandoned,
   154

Sutherland, Dwight, 112, 114*

Sutherland, John, 112

Sutherland family, 150

Sutherland Lumber Co., 112

"sweet Lucy" cheap wine, 107

Swift, James C., 83, 83*, 84

Swift & Company, 14, 53, 55, 92

Swift & Henry, 83, 86, 104, 128, 144

Swift & Henry office, 79*, 122

Swift & Henry Order Buying Company, 105,
   144

Symon, Bill and Sue, 111

T

Tailgate Ranch, 134

Texas
   first herd of longhorns driven north to, in
      1690, 4
   initial shipment of cattle to Kansas City from
      Abilene in 1867, 6
   overrun with longhorns after the Civil War, 4

Texas fever, disease caused by ticks, 77

Texas Longhorns, disappearing, 19

Theater Comique at the corner of 4th and
   Walnut, 18

Theis, Wayne, 155, 156

Thompson, Allen M., 97

To Tell the Truth program, 147

Toad-a-Loops gang, 47

Tom Mix hat, 59

"Town of Kansas," 141

Traders' Livestock Exchange, 34

train station, opened in 1878, 30

transportation, before the Civil War, 40

"Treasure in a Cornfield," by Greg Hawley, 5

truck shipments, grew with highway expansion,
   76

Trujillo, Rafael Leonidas, 127

Truman, Harry S, 108
   greeting a mule and its exhibitor, 109*
   letter to Fred Owen, 109*

Turkey Red winter wheat, 44

Turtle, Howard, 96, 155

Tuttle Creek dam, 119

U

Underground Railroad, route through the

bottoms, 143
Union Avenue, 22–23
Union Depot, 30, 30*, 55, 64
union organizers, received a hostile reception,
  107
Union Pacific Railway, 39
Union Station, 64, 64*
Union Stock Yards
  opened on June 1, 1871, 10–11
  replaced by "Kansas Stockyards," 12
unions, packing house laborers joining, 110
United Packinghouse Workers of America, 110
University of Missouri, veterinary medicine
  school, 146

V
Van Horn High School, 12
Van Horn, Robert T., 11–12
vaqueros (cowboys), first, 4
Vaughn, Joe H., 43
veterinarians, need for, 146

W
Wagstaff, Mr. and Mrs. Robert W., 150
Waldo, Kay, 141
Wayne, John, 136
Weil, Edgar, 95
well, in the West Bottoms, 21
West Bottoms
  business located in, 1
  described, 2
  flood protection, 117
  flooded in 1951, 117*
  future of, 150–154
  Irish families in, 20
  1907 map of, 3*
  removed from the 100-year flood plain, 122
  scoured for dead animals after 1951 flood,
    122
  smell of, 89
  as symbol of Kansas City, 22
  well, 21
West Bottoms fire, in 1917, 65–66
West End Hotel, 101, 136, 136*
West Side Feed Yards, 77
"wettest block in the world," on West 9th Street,
  23
wheat, dependable supply of, 44
Wheat, Eli, 130
Wheeler, Charles B., 142
whistle, Armour's, 15

William T. Kemper Fund., 150
Williams, Eddie, 113
Wilson Packing Co., left its plant, 118
Woodley, Mackey, 155
Worgul, Doug, 29, 143
World Series of Barbecue, 142, 146
World War I, mules in, 1
World War II
  glider and landing craft production, 103
  importance of Kansas City's agribusiness,
    103–106
  mules in, 148
Wyandots, distributed tribal lands, 51

Y
Yard Company, collection of old mounted steer
  horns, 129
"yard gait," 75
York, Clark's slave, 25